Know Your Y

Navigating the World of Work as a Millennial

Jordan M. Watson

In loving memory of my grandmother,

Georgia Bell McFarland

Includes bibliographical references and index.

Summary: A job-search manual designed to help millennials and young and experienced professionals navigate the world of work. Job search activities and exercises are included for additional assistance and self-reflection.

ISBN: 978-1719482837

Printed in the United States of America

First Edition

For information regarding special discounts for bulk purchases, please email <u>truenorthcareerconsulting@gmail.com</u> or visit tnorthcareerconsulting.com.

Contents

Introduction   4

The Purpose of this book   7

Disclaimer   9

Chapter 1: The Difference Between a Degree and a Piece of Paper   10
Making your degree meaningful.

Chapter 2: Yours is a New and Different Generation   22
Discovering the uniqueness of your generation.

Chapter 3: Who Are You?   40
Identifying what you bring to the workplace. Helping you define your skills, accomplishments and professional experiences.

Chapter 4: Discovering the Best Career Options for You   60
Exploring your industry of interest. Learning how to familiarize yourself with a company's' brand.

Chapter 5: Personal Branding   70
Marketing yourself effectively for the workplace. Learning how to leave a positive and lasting impression.

Chapter 6: Networking   84
Creating a solid network that lasts a lifetime.

Chapter 7: The Job Search   114
Developing an effective and efficient job search plan that yields successful results.

Chapter 8: Effective Interviewing: Bringing Your Best Game to the Interview   136
Preparation 101: Tips and strategies on how to have a successful interview.

Chapter 9: Job Acceptance and Negotiation   162
Accepting a job while still remembering your worth

Chapter 10: Surviving and Thriving in the First Ninety Days of Your Career   170
Surviving the 90-day probationary period.

Chapter 11: Just In Case That Wasn't Enough…   181
Budgets, credit history, retirement…oh my!

Final Word   191

Career Resources   192

Acknowledgements   194

Notes   196

About the Author   205

Index   206

Introduction

Hello, my name is Jordan and I am a millennial. And just like you, I am a millennial still trying to figure out this thing called life. I know sometimes we think we should already have all the answers. But we don't and it is more than okay to admit that. We're really just getting started so there's really no reason why we should even think having all the answers is an 'option' for us at this point in time. Besides, ask any Baby boomer you know and if they're being honest, they will tell you *they* don't even have all the answers. So if they don't….

I am also a millennial who is very confident in my skills and experience to this point, and I want you to be able to say the same. That is why I wrote this book. As for what qualifies me to do so…

I received a Bachelor of Arts and Science in Journalism with a concentration in Public Relations from Georgia State University in Atlanta, GA. I received a Master of Education in Clinical Mental Health Counseling from the University of Missouri- St. Louis in St. Louis, MO. I am also a Licensed Professional Counselor, Career Consultant, and an Etiquette Consultant with The Etiquette Institute.

I have nearly a decade of experience in presenting and developing workshops related to training and professional development as well as mentoring and coaching a variety of individuals and people-groups including college students, adult learners, and young professionals. I have obtained certifications in my profession such as the *DISC Assessment* and the *Myers Briggs Type Indicator*, which have both strengthened my experience in providing counseling and coaching services to others.

But again…I do NOT have all the answers and I'd be lying if I said I did. My life has definitely not been without its share of challenges, tears, fear, and anxiety. I've even failed at a few things along the way. I have doubted my worth and wondered if I would ever have enough experience to succeed and have questioned whether I am behind the 'curve' in comparison to my peers when it comes to successes and achievements. And if I am behind, would I ever catch up?

Every time I've found myself feeling like this, however, something happens (or I make something happen) to prove to me that my thoughts and fears are unfounded. I wish I could say that these experiences have taught me not to do this to myself, but I cannot. What can I say? I am human.

What I *can* say with confidence is that I know my worth and I know that I am destined for greatness…for *my* greatness. And so are you!

My confidence primarily comes from three sources: me, my mom, and my husband. When I take the time to look at myself and consider what I have already accomplished, I realize that everything I have done to this point is a stepping stone to what comes next and that I have what it takes to get there.

My mom's influence comes in the form of her voice inside my head telling me over and over again, "If there is a will there is always a way." Her words have given me the determination to set my sites on something and then do whatever I can or have to do to get there. Nothing illegal or harmful to others, of course, but you know what I mean. Instead of accepting defeat, learn, do some research, explore your options, and immerse yourself in uncovering your 'why', i.e. your purpose.

As for my husband, when I voiced my concern and angst over pursuing something new (like writing this book), he asked why I was having those feelings. My answer was simple: fear of falling flat on my face…of failing. Being the loving, gentle, man that he is (he really is), he looked at me and said, "If you fall, it's okay. You just get up, brush yourself off, and keep going."

Do you believe that? Do you believe you don't have to view defeat as failure? If so, then this book will serve to refuel your confidence and stamina so that you can continue to set and achieve your life goals. If you don't, you soon will.

FYI: Don't be surprised if your discoveries lead you in a different direction than where you thought you would be headed. Don't fight it. Just go with it because **it's not where you end up that makes you who you are, it's the journey you take to get there.**

The Purpose of this Book

As I stated in the preface, the purpose of this book is to help you learn how to discover and achieve your life goals (your 'why') one achievement at a time. As you move through the book you will come to realize that:

- Where you are now is where you are supposed to be…now.
- Where you are not is not where you are going to be…later.

All too often when talking with other millennials who are in the beginning stages of their career development process, the angst and nervous energy radiating from them is palpable. And the primary culprit in making them feel the way they do is something I call the "Social Media Syndrome".

The "Social Media Syndrome" is the name I've given to allowing yourself to be sucked into the not-so-real lives of your peers. Few of us put the unabridged, unembellished version of ourselves on any form of social media. Instead, we put the pictures and status updates we believe will get the most 'likes' and/or that make us appear as if we are living the dream large and in charge. We show and tell what we want people to know, or in many cases what we want them to *think*.

The same holds true for conversations you have with the people you graduated with (high school or college). Yes, your friends may have big plans and a great job or job offer waiting for them, but I'm willing to bet you may not have the full story. In other words, it is highly probable they are only sharing what a) they think will happen or b) what eventually happened. What they didn't do was share the challenges and detours they experienced to get there. And trust me, there are always challenges and almost-always a detour or two.

Maybe the great job or job offer is only great on paper. Maybe it's not what they really want to do or something they find truly fulfilling. Maybe their big plans are their attempt to recover from being passed over for a promotion or were forced upon them, per se, because they were fired from a job. In other words, you only know what they want you to know. So if you do not remember anything else from this book, please remember to **always be yourself and no one else** and that:

- **Where you are now is where you are supposed to be...now.**
- **Where you are not is not where you are going to be...later.**

This book is also meant to be used as a general reference point that you can use throughout the different stages and phases of your career—from the first resume submission and interview to the day you retire from the workforce. I know—that day seems light-years away, but from what I hear, the time passes more quickly than we think it will.

This book, however, WILL NOT provide you with a detailed approach or outline specifically tailored for your life. It's up to you to incorporate what you read and apply it to your individual situation. There is also no timeline to follow. For example, you will not read anything about the fact that obtaining a master's before you are twenty-five will make or break your career. Neither will you find anything about reaching specific investment goals by a certain age to guarantee financial security. These are your goals to set...or not. This book is simply meant to provide you with the **tools and processes you need to navigate YOUR professional (and private) life in the direction YOU want it to go.**

DISCLAIMER

Stories that are based on real-life situations have been included to make the book more enjoyable and relatable. The character names as well as the important demographic and geographic information are fictional for privacy and protection.

Chapter 1:

The Difference Between a Degree and a Piece of Paper

Have you ever been asked why you went to college? I have. And my answer was always "Why wouldn't I?" I never really considered college as optional. It was more of a natural next step. My grandmother was a teacher and principal for over thirty years. Both of my parents earned master's degrees. Pursuing an education beyond high school was…like I said, the natural next step for me. So the question of why I went was never difficult for me to answer. What I have had trouble with, however, is answering the question of how my degree really translates into my profession and the 'real world'.

Shakespeare said (via Juliet), "A rose by any other name would smell as sweet"; meaning that your paper degree, your paper birth certificate, your paper winning lottery ticket, and your paper grocery list are all just paper. Or are they?

When you look at your degree in its frame, prominently displayed for everyone's viewing pleasure, you see a whole lot more than a piece of paper. You see:

- Thousands of dollars spent on books, tuition, and all the other fees that come with a college education
- Countless (literally) hours of studying
- Memories made with friends you wouldn't trade for all the money in the world
- The emotional rollercoaster of stress, excitement, pride, self-doubt, and everything in between you rode non-stop for four (or more) years

- A sense of accomplishment mingled with anticipation for the future and even a sense of entitlement because of all the hard work that went into earning said degree

You see these things because you know what it took to get to it. I get that. But to be blunt, prospective employers don't really care about those things. To them your degree really is just a piece of paper. They are more interested in knowing what YOU have to offer. What did you *learn* and how will your newly-acquired knowledge and skills work for *them?*

Employers need you to be able to market your skills and knowledge to them via a resume and interview. In other words, you need to sell yourself (in a good way). There are some degrees that carry a bit more weight than others—nursing, for instance. Potential employers know that in order to obtain your degree you have to have successfully completed a good deal of clinical work. Marketing or biology on the other hand, don't require as much hands-on training prior to graduation, so you are going to have to work a little harder to get your foot in the proverbial door. Again…think of it as trying to sell the best product…YOU.

To help you understand how to go about presenting yourself this way, you need to dissect your degree into a variety of 'pieces' so that you can put together a more thorough and precise presentation of yourself. A sales pitch, per se.

Major

Certifications/License obtained (SAP, Teaching certificate, etc.)

Skills

Classes

Class projects/activities

Internships

Volunteer

Work Experience

Extracurricular Activities

Do you see how including these details gives you more credibility? You are more than just a name on a piece of paper. You are a person of action. From this list you can now begin to think about your own experiences and how they may apply to the positions you are seeking.

Now let's take it to the next level. Take a few minutes to do the following exercise to 'map out' your major; giving you the ability to create a visual aid that pinpoints what it is about your chosen major that most appeals to you. What direction would you like to take it in order to feed your passion? How do you want to use what you've learned to start your journey toward living a fulfilling and productive life in the workforce and in the real and very grownup world?

Complete the activity on the following pages to begin exploring how to apply your major to the workplace.

Mapping Your Major:

Making Your Major Work for You in the Workplace

STEP 1:

In the center of a piece of paper write the name of your major, certification, and/or license and draw a circle around it.

STEP 2:

Scatter the following words on your paper, drawing a circle around each one:

- **Courses Required**

- **Skills**

- **Possible Careers**

- **Interesting Items (famous people and world events pertaining to this field of study, advances made in the last decade, etc.)**

- **Knowledge**

- **Related Courses From Other Departments**

- **Internships**

STEP 3:

Jot down ideas related to each of the categories and draw circles around them as well. Write as much as you can, filling in everything you know about your chosen field of study and the possibilities that go with it.

STEP 4:

When you are done, take a step back and look at your map:

- **What pops out at you?'**

- **What is the most interesting part of the map to you? In other words, what "speaks" to you?**

- **How can you imagine connecting your major to a career/workplace?**

- **How have you tailored it to fit your interests?**

- **Did you take a series of courses that focused on a particular aspect of the major? Why? What did you enjoy about them?**

- **What skills did you learn**

- **Based on your answers, do you feel yourself being pulled in one particular direction over another in your field of study?**

- **Did this exercise provide the affirmation you needed that you are heading in the right direction for YOU, or did it pique your interest in taking your career in another direction?**

STEP 5:

Pull your thoughts together. What are the most important aspects of your major? If you had to identify three

characteristics you've developed or acquired from your major, what would they be?

1.

2.

3.

Now that you have taken the time to briefly analyze your major and where it can take you, I want you to go back and take another look at some of the things you read prior to completing the exercise. As you read through the following few pages, take time to really think about how these things apply to your own unique situation. In doing so you will be better equipped—both mentally and physically—to market yourself into a job that is where you are meant to be at this point in your life.

Oh, and one last thing before you continue…the degree you hold in your hands (or have hanging on your wall) is YOUR opportunity for an even better opportunity. For that matter, wherever you are right now is YOUR opportunity for an even better opportunity.

First things first…

Before you can expect a prospective employer to take you seriously, you have to take yourself seriously. You have to be able to answer the questions:

- Why you chose your particular degree program
- What you have to offer someone because of your degree

Without knowing the answers to these questions, you are going to have a difficult time convincing anyone you have much to offer.

IMPORTANT: Don't think this doesn't apply to you if you are one of the *many* college graduates who decide to take their career in a different or even opposite direction than what their degree would imply. Doing so doesn't automatically cancel out or invalidate the last four (or more) years of your life. And no matter what anyone tries to tell you, everything you've done has NOT been a complete waste of time, energy, and money.

Case in point: Emily P.

In high school, Emily was always the one making sure events were organized and that the details weren't overlooked. Yes, she knew so-and-so had agreed to secure donations from local businesses for prom and Project Graduation, but she didn't give them a chance to forget or slough off their responsibilities. She asked for a list of who was called and what was being donated. She also made sure it was picked up and that thank-you notes were written.

That's why it seemed only natural when she chose to pursue a degree in hotel and restaurant management and marketing. Halfway into her sophomore year, however, Emily started having doubts about what she was doing. She tried to push her feelings aside, but by junior year, she found she dreaded the classes and that she didn't like the interaction with the general public the way she thought she would. She was much more comfortable managing small groups of people she knew.

Emily thought long and hard her junior year. She didn't want to take the time or go into more debt—things that would be necessary if she changed her major. Instead, Emily took a deep breath, changed as many classes as possible to still be able to graduate on time, and decided to make the best of the situation and use what she could from her program to help her get a job in a field she had come to realize she truly enjoyed…business management.

Today, Emily is twenty-six and working as a department manager of a large bank. She oversees a group of about twenty employees and is highly respected by them and her superiors. She is happy, confident, and doesn't feel the least bit of remorse for changing her mind. She will also tell you that her degree was not a complete waste of anything.

"Nothing you do is a waste of time if you don't let it be. I use a lot of the management skills and relational skills I learned in the program. Realizing that I didn't have all the answers back then helped me grow up a lot. It made me think harder and gave me a greater sense of compassion for others."

I like what she said—that nothing you do is a waste of time if you don't let it be. The years you've just spent preparing for the next opportunity in your life has been a valuable investment in your future. Not only have you acquired specialized knowledge, you have acquired study skills, people skills, the ability to manage yourself, your time, and your priorities, and you have discovered that you are the only one ultimately responsible for your future.

Putting your degree to work for you

Knowing these things is not enough, though. You have to use what you know in order to get the most you can from your degree. Look back at the exercise you did on paper. What were those things that stood out to you? Pick a couple from each category and decide how they can work together to help you achieve your next goal. Remember: You worked hard for your degree. Now it's time to make it go to work for you.

Marketing yourself

In order to land the position you want you have to know a) what employers want to hear and b) how to share these things about yourself with them.

Remember, to them your degree is just paper and you are just one of hundreds (if not more) coming to them for a job. Therefore, you have to be able to tell them why AND how you spent the last several years working toward your degree and why it is not just a piece of paper. You need to let prospective employers see what you are capable of doing *because* you have your degree.

Jared and Christopher are two perfect examples of what this means. They both graduated from the same prestigious university with degrees in chemical engineering. Both had 4.0 GPAs. Jared, however, had also been part of a team that competed against chemical engineering programs from other universities on special projects. He also spent two summers interning with a small company. Christopher did neither. He chose to focus on taking summer classes in order to be able to graduate a full year earlier than his freshman class. He thought in doing so he was getting ahead of the game.

When both young men attended a job fair on campus early in their senior year, Jared was offered a position by three different companies. All three said that while his grades were impressive, it was his drive to actually be a part of his field of study that made him so desirable. Christopher left having no offers and only one possible interview. Two prospective employers did offer him an internship—something he should have already done.

Getting ahead of the game, as Christopher put it, isn't just about academics. It's also about taking steps to use what you are learning while you are still learning. It's about being…not just doing.

So how do you do that? By:

- Recognizing what your degree can actually contribute to an employer: How will your skills and knowledge make the workplace better, more cutting-edge, put them ahead of their competitors, increase the bottom line….
- Selling these attributes to prospective employers on your resume, personal interviews, and references

What you have done is commendable. An education doesn't just happen. It takes hard work and dedication, so don't do yourself the injustice of settling for less than you can have. You've worked hard for your degree, so I'll say it again…**now it is time to let your degree work for you.**

Chapter 2:

Yours Is A New And Different Generation

My grandmother worked as a teacher and a principal for over 30 years. My mom has worked for the same corporation for over 40 years. My dad has worked in the nonprofit sector for over 25 years and my uncle has been an engineer for over 35 years. 41% of millennials expect to be in their current job for two years or less compared to 17% of Gen X and 10% of Boomers. Notice the difference?

These statistics show that the career development of a millennial is a journey not a destination. It is an ongoing process rather than a result of previous processes (education). Research also supports that the millennial generation will transition into various jobs and careers over the course of their 'work life'.

It hasn't always been this way

Every generation stakes its claim in respect to the impact it makes and the changes they birth into society.

The Greatest Generation are those who were young adults through middle-age during WWII. They are also referred to as Traditionalists. They were the men and women who were raised with the standard of keeping their nose to the grindstone, so to speak. Their work ethic was iron-clad and could not be shaken. They prided themselves on their 'stick to it' attitude—choosing a career path and sticking with it unless doing so became impossible.

They were (and still are) a conservative generation who worked best under an organized chain of command and who gave and sought respect and appreciation for a job well done and the experience they brought to the table.

These men and women are to be admired and respected because it was their work ethic that allowed them to survive the Great Depression with as much dignity as possible and to withstand the horrors of WWII (both on the battlefield and here at home). They are the generation that ensured the freedoms we enjoy today—the freedoms that have allowed the generations that came after them (including you) to do their thing.

The Baby Boomers are those born between 1946 and 1964. They are the product of love reunited after WWII and the Korean Conflict. They are a generation that was raised to work hard and do your best—to respect and appreciate the enormous cost of the rights and freedoms they had. Their homes were relatively happy and conservative ones in which Dad went to work and Mom stayed home to care for the house and family.

As for their entry into adulthood and the workforce, Baby Boomers focused on developing careers through opportunities within one organization or industry. Their intentions were to move up the ladder based on seniority, even if that seniority didn't always mean they were the most skilled & qualified for the position.

Like their parents, Baby Boomers were and still are most comfortable with a clear-cut chain of command. But unlike their parents, they were looking for a pleasant and enjoyable work atmosphere to go with it. Being friends as well as co-workers was something they were after.

This is also the group that saw a voluntary surge in women entering the workforce. Women in the previous generation had to go to work to fill the void left by the hundreds of thousands of men overseas. They had to support their families in their husband's absence. And for those whose husband didn't come home, they remained the primary 'bread winner'. But many Baby Boomer women wanted to work. Many were drawn to what they viewed as the excitement and allure of a career outside the home. These women were going to college and wanted to put their education to good use and wanted to be treated equally to men. They wanted more but didn't really know what 'more' was and because these were unchartered waters, for most women it wasn't nearly as exciting and fun as they thought it would be.

The movie, *9 to5* is a great (and funny) example of what I'm talking about. A single mom, a newly-divorced housewife, and a woman trying to climb the ladder of success all trying to make their way. While some of the obstacles they faced were hilarious and seemed downright unrealistic, they were actually comedic exaggerations of what women were actually up against. Women who were highly qualified and capable in their chosen field had to prove themselves job-wise AND person-wise.

The hardest part of all was the fact that they weren't just proving these things to their employer. They also had to prove it to themselves. Never before in this country had women had so many options. It was great—but with those options came a whole lot of role redefinition and juggling of responsibilities. Women were still moms and wives. That wasn't going to change and for the most part they didn't want it to. But figuring out how to have it all was a lot harder than it looked in their mind's eye and just like a lot of other things; it wasn't nearly as grand as they thought it would be.

Women weren't the only ones with problematic issues, though. Men suddenly found themselves having to change the way they worked and thought. And they had to learn how to handle women in the workplace.

As a millennial, you cannot truly understand or comprehend what this was like for them. But it wasn't easy. It wasn't easy because there were no established 'rules for the game'. These men had been brought up to treat women gently and chivalrously. Even those women who worked outside the home prior to this 'explosion' of women in the work force expected to be treated in this manner. But not *these* women.

These women wanted equality. They didn't want the door held open for them. They expected to be treated like one of the guys when it came to drinks after work or talking about sports and the stock market. They wanted to prove they were just as capable as their male counterparts. They wanted to prove there was no difference between men and women. But because there ARE differences between men and women, much of the time things didn't go so well.

Time and experience has been a great teacher, though. Well, those things and the perseverance of the determined and visionary Baby Boomers. They kept on going; bringing us to where we are today.

The next generation is known as **Generation X.** These are the adults born between the years of 1965 and 1980. This is the generation that saw the most radical changes in how work is done from a technological standpoint, but who have had the fewest personal issues to deal with in the work force.

Generation X workers have enjoyed the smooth waters that came after the storm weathered by the Baby Boomers. The Generation X worker is after a work-related challenge to keep them on their toes and to keep things interesting and stimulating, but they don't want anything less than a calm, relaxed, and enjoyable work atmosphere.

The Generation X worker is really the first generation we've looked at to be proactive in their career development in regard to not having any deep feelings of loyalty to a particular company or organization. They are going to go where they (the individual) need to go in order to reach the top. They are also the generation that wholeheartedly embraces higher education beyond a bachelor's degree. A master's and doctorate were often the goal in order to reach the summit of their field.

And finally, we have arrived at us…the **Millennials.** Millennials are those of us born between the years of 1981 and 2000. We are a workforce that is looking for flexibility, diversity, an atmosphere that is relaxed and enjoyable to spend time in, and we want the freedom to be creative in our own way.

We thrive on 'experiences'. In some ways I feel millennials have had more experiences than previous generations. We are more mobile than previous generations. We have access to more of the world than previous generations. We have had more opportunities and exposure to just about everything than previous generations. Because this is true, we've come to expect it and aren't comfortable without it.

Millennials are also approval-seekers. We want and need continual feedback from our superiors and our co-workers. This stems in part from the fact that we have been raised in a time where children are given participation trophies and are praised whether we've really earned it or not. We have a need to be recognized and if the company or organization we work for doesn't fulfill that need we see no reason to stay. After all, we are working to fulfill our goals and dreams, so if that isn't happening we need to change directions or paths so it will.

Let me say that again…we millennials view our job/career as a means to making our dreams come true and meeting our personal goals. This differs from past generations in the fact that by and large, a job/career was a means of sustenance and providing the resources for pursuing their goals and dreams.

Another way to say it would be like this: In previous generations, a job or career was what that person did. To a millennial, it is who they are.

Ours is a generation like none other. Part of the reason for this is the fact that the world is changing almost daily—thanks to our innovation and creativity. These changes are like nothing the world has seen or experienced before and we want to make sure we make the most of everything that is out there for us.

Each one was a step to where we are today

Without the tenacity, unyielding loyalty, and do-or-die work ethic of the Greatest Generation, it is both fair and safe to say that our country wouldn't exist. At least not in the way we know it. Had they not refused to give up and clawed their way out of the Depression, they might not have fought so diligently to preserve our freedoms in WWII. But they did, and because of that, they established an element of reverent pride and treated their very personal investment in our country with unparalleled love and respect. Without them we would have nothing.

The Greatest Generation's legacy was passed on to their children—the Baby Boomers—but because they didn't live through the experiences of their parents and grandparents, the attitude of the Baby Boomers softened a bit. The strong work-ethic was still there as was the attitude of loyalty and respect for authority. But they had a need and a desire to make their own mark on society. The mark they left was called 'change'. The Baby Boomers are responsible for cracking open the doors and windows that make it possible for us to be where we are today. They made it acceptable and even expected for women to not only be in the workplace, but to be in charge. Baby Boomers also gave us the courage to change things up even when it's not easy.

Generation X kept the changes coming and smoothed things out a bit. They also made it acceptable to make the workplace a pleasant and enjoyable place to be. Generation Xers were the ground-breakers of internet and computer technology—something we can no longer imagine being without. They also started the shift away from company loyalty to 'me loyalty'. They were the first generation to really begin seeing their job/career as an extension of who they are as people outside the workplace.

Pride (the good kind), respect, courage to change, and the realization that the way we spend most of our waking hours (job/career) are the things we've gotten from the generations before ours. They are all valuable and they are all part of the reason we have the mindset to pursue our goals and dreams as boldly and unashamedly as we do.

Life-long learners

We millennials are life-long learners. This isn't to say those from previous generations didn't (and don't) embrace learning new things. The other day I heard a great story on the radio. A wife and mom of eight children entered medical school at the age of fifty-five or six. With her husband's help and full support, she completed her education (she'd gotten her pre-med done online prior to this time) and the two of them started a clinic in a rural area of one of the southern states that was extremely poverty-stricken. So as you can see, we millennials don't have the corner on the market of being life-long learners, but society in general hasn't seen a generation like ours in which learning plays a major role in everyday life in a very long time.

Knowing this about yourself will hopefully make it easier for you to be at peace with the fact that along your career journey, it is quite possible that your career interest may change. As you continue to grow and develop throughout the years, you may encounter the need and desire to go in an entirely different direction than you are headed now.

Twists and turns are often part of the process

Olivia is a great example of this. The twists and turns she's taken since graduating from high school in 2006 rival the switchback roads in Arizona's Salt River Canyon, but each one has taken her exactly where she needed to be at the time.

Olivia came from a family that was well-known and highly respected in the farming/agricultural industry in the Midwest. She loved her 'farming roots' and had every intention of pursuing a career in the field of agriculture (no pun intended). But less than a semester into her freshman year in college, however, Olivia realized that while she loved the farm life, she wasn't the least bit interested in some of the other things that were involved in her degree program. Her disinterest showed in her grades and her attitude.

Unsure about what to do, Olivia focused on getting her general credits out of the way. She thought about doing a lot of different things—even the possibility of becoming a professional welder. It was something she was good at and enjoyed, but after thinking about it she decided she wasn't quite up to bucking what was a very male-dominant profession.

Things outside of school happened that caused her to end up in an entirely different location and not in school. She did, however, have an excellent job with an engineering company that worked closely with NASA and other US-friendly space programs (among other things).

Olivia's boss saw a lot of potential in her and quickly took the necessary steps to get her back in school to complete her bachelors (at the expense of the company) as well as several certifications; qualifying her to work in the field of aeronautic engineering. Olivia couldn't have been happier with her career choice.

She also met her husband in the process, so all in all life was about as perfect as she could have hoped it to be…until she and her husband adopted their newborn son. Olivia and her husband had been to hell and back (figuratively speaking, of course) during the adoption process. So when it came time to go back to work she couldn't stand the thought of leaving her son with someone else.

Becoming a mom suddenly made everything else pale in comparison. At this point Olivia's career path took yet another turn to the one marked STAY AT HOME MOM. Being a SAHM has been a perfect fit for Olivia's family. She was brought up in this same type of home, so it felt natural and right to her. But her little boy is almost five and Olivia knows that it won't be long before she will have her days to herself again. This has caused her to think about how she wants to spend them and begin weighing her options.

Her husband's job took them to a different part of the country; making it impossible for her to return to her former job. Even if she could, though, she says she doubts she would.

"I don't regret one choice I've made," she says, "because each one took me to the next phase in my life and except for a few stupid choices I made early-on in my college career, I always felt I was exactly where I was supposed to be at that particular time of my life."

When I asked her what was next, she laughed and said, "I'm going back to what I've always loved best—farming. Well, sort of. I've recently become a licensed and certified wildlife rehabilitator, which means I now work with the conservation agents to treat and care for injured or abandoned wildlife until it can be re-introduced back into its natural habitat."

Have you been counting? Or maybe you lost count. But between the ages of seventeen (when she graduated from high school) and twenty-eight (which is how old she is now) Olivia has taken six major job/career changes. Six in eleven years.

Olivia's journey may seem dizzying to some and even careless or haphazard to others. Still others are probably thinking that Olivia is your kindred spirit—that you two might have even been separated at birth because you are so much alike.

Seeing change as exploration

Like Olivia, your career goals may change once, twice, or several times. THAT IS OKAY. Because our world and the way we do business has undergone so many changes in the last few years (and shows no signs of slowing down), making these career changes is a lot like going on a career exploration. In career exploration, the goal is not necessarily to choose one for life, but to explore the things you are interested in doing and learning more about.

Your exploration process needs to be one in which you are fully engaged; meaning you give it one-hundred percent so that you will know whether or not it is a stepping stone to something else or the place you want to land. Research the field. Network to see where the job can take you. Job shadow before you make a commitment to eliminate the possibility of wasting an employer's time in hiring and training you. Intern to see if you have what it takes to do what is expected of you. Immerse yourself until you have the necessary information needed to make a decision.

Exploration isn't the same as irresponsibility

I feel I need to take a few minutes to explain the difference between career twists and turns and career exploration vs. irresponsibility or laziness. And yes, there is a difference…a big one.

Using Olivia as an example again, Olivia wasn't being irresponsible or lazy. She will admit she could have and should have tried harder during that first semester of college, but other than that, she gave one-hundred percent to everything else she did. She didn't quit when the going got tough or when she didn't want to do what was expected of her. She didn't quit because she thought she was being treated unfairly or because she got bored or didn't get the praise she thought she deserved. Each time she left one position for another, it was because the change was truly in her best interest. Each one was made only after putting a good deal of thought into it.

The same should be true for you, as well. It is draining on an employer to put the time and money into training you only to have you quit as soon as things don't go your way.

Another point of consideration is benefits. When you change career paths or even the company or organization you work for, you run the risk of losing important benefits such as health insurance and retirement. Now I know you think retirement is light years away and that you are as healthy as a horse so insurance isn't something you need to worry too much about, but you are wrong. Time passes much quicker than you think it will and accidents and illnesses sneak up on you and catch you unaware so you need to be prepared.

This isn't meant to be a contradiction of what I've already said about career twists and turns being okay. They *are* okay…when done for the right reasons and when done right. And in this case, 'right' means:

- Achieving a goal you have set for yourself
- Done with respect for the people you are working for and with
- Thought and planning are put into the action being taken and changes being made
- You aren't making changes simply for the sake of making changes

REMEMBER: Any twists and turns on your career path should lead you to a new 'better' or a new 'right'…for you.

Exploration is not always necessary

Before we change subjects I want to say one more thing about career paths and journeys….

In the same way making changes is okay, so is NOT making changes. If you are a millennial who:

- Knows exactly what you want to do with the rest of your life…then do it and don't let anyone make you feel you are missing out on anything because you don't feel the need to try something different
- Desires the kind of job stability that comes with pledging your loyalties to one particular company for possibly your entire career
- Feels comfortable working in a more traditional setting with traditional rules, office etiquette, etc.

Then by all means…do it!

Elizabeth announced to the 'world' at the age of nine that she was going to grow up to be a nurse who took care of babies. Twenty-two years later she is doing just that and has been since the week after she graduated from nursing school almost ten years ago. She can't imagine being anything but a nurse.

So remember…making changes in your career over the years is fine…even normal, for this millennial generation.

Exploring Your Options

Activity

Answer the following questions to help you decide whether career exploration is for you.

1. **Why did you choose the career path you are currently on?**

2. **How satisfied are you with the career choices you have made to this point?**

3. **How likely is it that you will be in your current career (not position) five years from now? Ten years?**

4. **How do the answers to question three make you feel?**

5. **If you could choose another career, what would it be?**

6. **Why?**

7. **Do you view changing career paths as being weak or indecisive? Why or why not?**

Complete the following exercise to help you see that changes are part of the process of growth and maturity.

MY FAVORITE WAYS TO SPEND MY TIME:

When I was 5 years old:

When I was 10 years old:

When I was 15 years old:

Now:

THE THINGS I CARE MOST ABOUT:

When I was 5 years old:

When I was 10 years old:

When I was 15 years old:

Now:

MY BIGGEST WORRIES/CONCERNS:

When I was 5 years old:

When I was 10 years old:

When I was 15 years old:

Now:

MY GOALS AND DREAMS FOR THE FUTURE:

When I was 5 years old:

When I was 10 years old:

When I was 15 years old:

Now:

Things sure can change over the course of a few years, can't they? And they're not done yet. If you were to ask your parents and grandparents to complete this same exercise and include 'when I was 30, 40, 50…' you would see that your primary focuses and concerns are going to continue to shift and turn. That's life. So don't be afraid to make changes IF that's what your gut is telling you to do. Just make them wisely.

Chapter 3:

Who Are You?

How many times as a kid were you asked, "What do you want to be when you grow up?" If you were like me the answer you gave depended on what you were being exposed to at the time. A great example of this can be seen during and after the Olympics.

During and after the Olympic games there is a huge increase in enrollments in swimming, skating, hockey, gymnastics, and running lessons/clubs for children. The same concept can be seen when it comes time for children to choose who they want to 'be' for Halloween. It's all about exposure or what is most popular at the time.

Now here's another question for you: How close are you to being what you said you wanted to be?

My undergraduate degree was in journalism with a concentration in public relations and a minor in marketing. But during those four years, if you asked me what my career goal was, I did not have a clue. What's more, by the time I reached my senior year, I was pretty confident that neither journalism nor marketing was a good fit for me.

I had explored all of the mainstream options for people in my soon-to-be profession. Television, radio, different facets of the business world…even medicine and law. I quickly eliminated medicine, though, because I don't do well around blood and well, that's kind of a big deal in the field of medicine.

That left me with two top contenders for my professional life—law and business. Knowing that gave me the answer I needed to the question of what I wanted to do with my major. I wanted to use it as a stepping stone to an MBA and JD. It was an easy answer to give—one that sounded great and made perfect sense. But even though I could say it, I didn't really believe it. I believed my answer to be the right one because I saw it as the pathway to one of two careers that were equally respectable. Either way, I would be considered a success. But while they are both considered successful careers, I never really saw myself being successful *in them*. They weren't me. They didn't fit…me.

Please do not misinterpret what I am trying to communicate to you by telling you this. Pursuing an MBA and a JD is worthy of respect and admiration. They both open a number of doors for opportunities that can bring a lifetime of professional and personal gratification. So if either or both of these degrees are of interest for you, DO IT. They just weren't for me.

What is work

The word 'work' has numerous synonyms including: labor, task, job, occupation, vocation, grind, effort, exertion, production, creation, masterpiece, toil effort, and operate.

As you looked through the list, did you notice how some have a negative connotation while others are more positive and upbeat? I can personally relate to this because growing up and clear up to the time I was in college, my perception of work could pretty much be described as a job, task, or an occupation. It was what you did to make a living. I also viewed work as something that was a given or natural next step after receiving a college education. Education followed by work. That was what life was all about.

And it is…fundamentally. But work is, or should be, about a lot more than something you labor at or exert yourself (body, mind, or both) to do. So ask yourself this: **What is your perception of work?**

To help you answer that question, circle the three words from the first paragraph of this section that best describe your views of your work. Did you circle words that put a more positive or negative spin on the word? Now take a few minutes and use the space below to make a few notes as to why you chose the words you did.

Notes:

Is this the perception of work you want to carry with you throughout your career?

Who are you

In order to achieve the greatest degree of satisfaction and fulfillment from your work you need to understand who you are, how you identify with yourself in relation to the job world, and how your feelings about your work influences the overall meaning and level of satisfaction you have in your life. To help you do that, let's go back a few years to help you see how and why you view yourself the way you do…

For many of us, high school was a period of emotional and transitional chaos. Not only were we dealing with that awkward period of being stuck between a child and adult, we were having a new and bigger 'set' of expectations put on us. We were told by teachers, advisors, and parents to start giving serious thought to what we wanted to be "when we grew" up *and* that we needed to start putting together a plan of how to get there *and* to put that plan into motion. College, trade school, or the military were the three most common options encouraged by most schools. And once you chose one of those options, you spent the rest of high school trying to make it happen.

For those who chose to extend their education by going to a college, university, or trade school, it was okay not to have the *details* of your post-graduation plan laid out. You didn't even have to know for certain what you wanted to major in, but you were expected to select a 'good school' and make sure your GPA, extra-curricular activities, and behavior would be adequate to get you in. However, by the time senior year rolled around, you were expected to have a pretty solid post-graduation plan in place.

Choosing the military was an option that for the most part took care of things for you. You enlisted, chose your MOS (method of service)—usually under the advisement of the recruiter—and then on the appointed day, you were sworn into active duty. From there it was boot camp and then whatever specialized training was required for the job you would be doing.

For those students who did not pursue either option (college or military), they were left to decide their future on their own. But in many cases there really weren't many decisions to be made due to the lack of options for blue-collar or entry-level jobs.

No matter which direction you went (or are currently going), the expectations are there for you to have your future plans laid out and the pressure is on for you to succeed in that plan.

- You are pressured to choose something that will result in a "high" paying job, or a comfortable lifestyle.
- If you choose the college route, you are pressured to stick with your major even if you are no longer interested in it just so you can graduate in four years.
- You are pressured to have your whole life figured out by the time you are twenty-two, even though that is statistically less than one-third of your life!

Looking at it in black and white, it is easy to see why so many of us had, or are having trouble figuring out who we are when it comes to our perception of work. With all the stress of meeting everyone else's expectations it is easy to get sucked into something that isn't a good fit for you. It doesn't help that as a society we tend to measure someone's worth by their education, their job, and their lifestyle. But this is neither fair nor accurate because what would be viewed as a *vocation* (calling) to you, may be more like a grind or labor to someone else.

You need to derive your own perception of work and how it defines and influences your life and personality. You need to be the one to do that—not someone else.

Be true to yourself

Franklin and Kelly were high school sweethearts. Kelly planned to go to college to become an elementary school teacher—something she had wanted to do since sixth grade. Franklin knew what he wanted to do with his life, but everyone (including Kelly) tried to dissuade him.

What was it Franklin wanted to do? He wanted to go to mortuary school and become a licensed funeral director. Franklin had lost his mom and grandma in a car accident when he was only ten, but he had never forgotten the way the people at the funeral home had treated him, his dad, his three sisters, and his grandpa. They were so kind and went out of their way to try to help them. But that was a job for 'weird' and 'nerdy' people everyone told him. He could do much better than that.

Franklin liked to cook, so he listened to everyone else and went to trade school to become a chef. Cooking became a chore instead of a hobby he enjoyed. He knew before he graduated that this was not what he wanted to do for the rest of his life. Next he tried selling real estate. Nope, that wasn't it either. Next Kelly's dad suggested he go into law enforcement. Franklin wanted to help people and being a police officer allowed you to do that and earn a good living.

Franklin couldn't argue with logic like that, so he entered the law enforcement academy. Three weeks later he dropped out. There was no way he would ever be able to draw his weapon on someone. That wasn't who he was.

At this point Franklin felt like a failure. Kelly assured him he wasn't a failure—that he was just having trouble figuring out what he wanted to do with his life.

"I know exactly what I want to do," Franklin told her. "I've know what I want to do for years. It's you and everyone else that can't come to grips with it. But you know what? I don't care anymore. I'm tired of trying to meet everyone else's expectations. I'm going to mortuary school so I can have career I know I'll be good at and enjoy instead of just some job I go to every day to pay the bills."

Kelly apologized over and over for having made him feel like what he wanted to do wasn't good enough and promised to never make him feel like that again.

Six years later, Franklin is co-owner of a funeral home and is highly respected in the industry and by the people of the community. Kelly taught third grade until she gave birth to twins two years ago. Today she is a stay-at-home mom who prefers private tutoring to being in the classroom.

Franklin knew how he wanted his perception of work to affect his life, but it wasn't until he had the courage to be himself that he was able to do what he knew was right…for him.

The junction of work and life

Understanding your perception of work on a personal level requires you to be true to yourself on your 'journey' of self-discovery. You need to feel free to pursue the career path that you feel will bring you the most satisfaction and fulfillment on the job. But job satisfaction and fulfillment isn't all you need to consider when deciding which career path to take. You also need to consider how your career path will impact your life beyond nine to five.

You need to ask yourself:

- What type of life do you actually want to live?
- How does your education and concept of work relate to your desired lifestyle?

- Where did you come from? In other words, who has influenced your life and the decisions you've made thus far? What experiences have brought you to this point in your life?
- Where do you want to go? Are you actively pursuing the path to get there?

In answering these questions you will be able to better understand how your current situation lines up with where you want to go AND how to make any adjustments necessary to make sure you get there.

My Personal Timeline
Activity

Purpose: When you take the time to look at your life as a whole, themes often emerge that can lead you toward the career best suited for you. The goal of this activity is to help you do just that by thinking about the people, events, and experiences that have shaped you into the person you are and into the person you are on your way to becoming.

What to do: Draw a horizontal line on a piece of paper. At the left end of the line, mark your birth date. At the other end, put today's date. This line will present your Personal Timeline

Make marks on the line and label them accordingly to denote major events, accomplishments, activities, work and personal experiences that have impacted your identity and future goals.

Reflection Questions: Answer the following questions about your timeline:

- What did you learn about yourself? What surprised you?
- What themes emerged? How do you see these themes continuing 5 years from now?
- Who were the important people in your life? How are they currently impacting your life?
- Describe the high points on your lifeline? What made those points so positive?
- Describe the low points on your lifeline? What made those points so negative?
- How do you see your timeline impacting your career decision-making?
- At the low points, what actions did you take to make things better to address the situation?
- At times when things were turning down, what might you

have done differently to rectify the situation?

Mapping My Life
Activity

Purpose: Mapping the interesting, exciting, and significant things you've done in your life in order to determine how you got to where you are now.

What to do: Write down all of the interesting, exciting, and significant things you've done, or that have happened in your life to this point. Go back as far as your memory will allow and remember: this is YOUR life-map. Anything YOU think is interesting, exciting, or significant is. So write it down. Keep it simple—a word, phrase, symbol, picture…whatever.

For example: Have you had unique jobs or taken unusual classes? Did you have a memorable summer experience? What are you most proud of? Do you have hobbies you've pursued and enjoy? What honors have you earned? Did you face a tough challenge? What successful experiences can you recall?

Don't worry about listing them in order. In fact, the more randomly you place them on the paper the better it will be for this exercise. Once you're done it is time to begin analyzing your map.

- Begin to connect (by drawing lines) the obvious links. For example, if you have a lot of sports-related things written down, connect all the different sports.
- After you've made all the connections between the different things you have done, look for and list all the commonalities between the different lines. For example, were most of the things team events or individual accomplishments? Were you a leader? Were you highly competitive? Were they mainly academic? Artistic? Athletic? Were you satisfied
- Now it's time to connect all the dots of the commonalities. What are the connecting themes or threads that run through

- your lives? Do you seem to use certain skills over and over again?

The answers to these questions will help you better understand how you got to where you are right now and can guide you onto a career path that is best-suited to your personality and your perception of work and how you want it to affect your life outside of the time you spend on the job.

The Present State of You

The following questions are a continuation of the previous exercise. In answering them, you will be 'forced' to see your life through a realistic lens, which will then help you discern whether you want to continue on your current path or take a different one.

Skills

What are you good at?

What skills did you learn in the process of earning your degree? What classes did you take to strengthen those skills?

**Skills can be broken down into 2 categories: Soft and Hard or Transferable and Industry- Specific. Hard skills are those skills that are very specific to your field of interest. They are typically more technical in nature. Soft (or transferrable skills) are those skills that many employers look for in a potential candidate. Transferrable skills represent "How" you are going to do your job. Examples include leadership, communication, and interpersonal skills. Transferrable skills make it easier to transition from one workplace to another because many employers look for these skills.*

Interests

What do you like to do?

What excites you?

What activities would you be interested in doing even if you weren't being compensated for them?

Workplace Values

What do you believe are the most important ethical values in the workplace?

What do you want your work environment to look like?

What are your non-negotiable's in a work environment. In other words, what would cause you to leave?

Personality Preferences

What kind of work environment would be a natural fit for your personality? (Do you like working in a team, by yourself, or a combination of both? Describe the ideal leadership style of your next supervisor?)

What are some of your observable behaviors? (How would others describe you? How would you describe yourself?)

Strengths

What are your strengths from a character and personality perspective?

What activities/tasks are effortless for you?

What personal traits have you received compliments for?

Weaknesses

What are your character or personality weaknesses?

What are skills that you can demonstrate effectively but drain your energy?

Short-term & Long-term goals

What are you striving towards? (2-5 years? 10 years?)

Self-worth

How do you define your worth? Would you invest in yourself? Do you believe that you have what it takes to be successful? Explain.

The Future State of You

What do you want the overall impact of your life to be? For example, do you have a need and desire for a prestigious career or are you more concerned with the humanitarian impact your life will have on others? Are you more interested in the impact your career will have on others or on your bank account? To what extent do you believe your personality is or should be connected to your professional life?

How well do the answers to the questions in The Present State of You line up with the answers to the questions in the above paragraph?

Having a sense of satisfaction and feeling successful in your career is important. Helping you achieve that is the primary purpose of this book. But because your work identity is only a part of your true and total self, it is important to understand the correlation between your career and your personal life. Who we are at work determines our career growth, but who we are in life determines our personal growth and they both play a key role in our happiness.

Who I want to be
Activity

Picture yourself a few years down the road. What vision do you have for your future?

NOTE: Don't limit yourself to occupational titles or career fields; instead, provide detailed descriptions of what you'd like to be doing, where you'd like to live, who you'd like to spend time with, and what special skills, training or interests you would hope to explore and develop.

Your mission statement

A mission statement is defined as: "A formal summary of the aims and values of a company, organization, or individual".

Mission statements aren't just for business or organizations, though. YOU can have a mission statement, too. Writing a personal mission statement is an excellent method of self-accountability and motivation. So guess what you're going to do next? That's right—you're going to write your personal mission statement.

I'm going to make it somewhat easy for you, though, by giving you a list of questions to answer. Once you answer the questions with short, simple answers, go back and write the answers in complete sentences on a separate piece of paper; adding in the details where appropriate. When you are done you will have personal mission statement. Answer the following questions below and then write your statement.

NOTE: When writing your mission statement, write it as if a prospective employer has just said, "Tell me about yourself." Tell me why I should hire you to work for me."

- Who am I?
- What are my morals and beliefs?
- What people and things do I value most in this life and why?
- What do I want to accomplish in my personal life?
- What do I want to accomplish in my career life?
- How do I want people to see me?
- What do I want people to remember me for—what contributions do I want to make to the world (even if the world is 'just' the people around me)?

Now that you know who you are, it's time to move forward another step and start getting serious about finding out which career path is the right one for you.

Chapter 4:

Discovering the Best Career Options for You

Shortly after I graduated from college I decided to give journalism a shot. It was, after all, what my major was in. What did it matter that I had no long-range plans to make journalism my life's work? What did it matter that my heart wasn't in it? I had the degree so I needed to use it, right? Besides, writing for a big fashion magazine *did* sound pretty exciting. And in order for that to happen, I'd 'have' to move to NY City…which also sounded exciting, so what did I have to lose?

When I told a friend of mine what I wanted to do—that I wanted to move to New York and write for a fashion magazine, he was actually willing and able to help me connect with another one of his friends who just happened to be pursuing a similar position.

I will never forget the conversation I had with her because it was by far the absolute worst conversation I had ever had or *will* ever have with anyone on a professional level. I was extremely unprepared and quite honestly I sounded like a silly teenager. I'm not kidding—it was awful.

After exchanging pleasantries, she immediately asked me why I was interested in journalism and in writing for a profession. When I did not have a direct response to her question, she proceeded to try to get more out of me by asking me the following questions, "What do you know about the job market in New York?" What are some magazines or publications you find interesting—that you feel you would enjoy working for—and could make a positive contribution to with your work?" "What designers are you most interested in?"

My standard answer was, "Uh…….uh…….." followed by fumbling

and flailing words that made no sense and that did *not* answer her questions.

See…I told you it was the worst conversation ever!

But as awful as it was, it wasn't a complete waste of time and oxygen. I learned a very valuable (and costly) lesson that day. I learned that I would do whatever was necessary to never put myself in that position again…ever. I would begin researching the career options available to me based on my degree so that I would a) know what paths I might want to pursue and b) be able to provide knowledgeable and cognizant answers to questions asked by professional contacts and potential employers. I want to also strongly advise you to do the same.

Researching your career interest(s) is a benefit to both you and prospective employers. Doing so gives you the chance to determine what career options available within your field most interest you; letting you know what kind of job you need to be searching for. It also eliminates putting yourself in the position I put myself in— being completely unprepared to discuss a possible position. Knowing these things also shows a potential employer that you are genuinely interested in working for them. Being able to answer questions as they pertain to the particular position you are interviewing for AND to their company earns you major points with your interviewer. Researching your possible career options also demonstrates your confidence and expertise in a given field.

How to research your career options

Researching your career options isn't as technical or ominous as it sounds. Some people might even refer to it as 'thinking outside the box' when deciding how to use your degree. So for the next few pages, that's what we are going to do.

What areas of your industry interest you

I cannot think of any job out there that doesn't have a variety of opportunities for employment. Think about it…

- Doctors have the option of general practice, OB/GYN, cardiologist, or almost countless other specialties.
- Biologists can work in a lab, a zoo, as a teacher, or in the agricultural field (to name a few).
- Teachers can choose the grade and subject they teach.
- Journalists can work on a magazine, a newspaper, web journalism, television, or radio. They can be news reporters, food critics, fashion reports, write special-interest articles (parenting, marriage, decorating, etc.), write technical documents, or any number of other things.
- Secretaries can choose to work in the industry that most appeals to them.
- Business and finance majors have an endless list of options.

Your job is to decide which one(s) interest you most. You should be able to do this without too much trouble by following this simple plan:

- List the options that are of no interest to you and cross them off your possible jobs list.
- List any area that piques your interest on any level.
- Study the list you just made and start placing them in order of importance or order of most-desirable to least-desirable.

See, that' wasn't so hard was it? Besides, this doesn't have to be the Magna Carta of your career path. It is simply a reasonable method to get you headed in the right direction with the fewest possible detrimental detours, aka disastrous phone calls. Taking this somewhat calculated approach to mapping out possible jobs in your chosen field also saves time and a great deal of emotional and mental fatigue. Trust me when I say it is no fun applying and being turned down for a job. Being rejected hurts and eats away at your sense of confidence and self-worth whether you actually wanted or were well-suited for the job or not.

I think we will readily agree that this stage of our lives is stressful enough without adding to it unnecessarily. So why not do something simple, yet effective to reduce the amount of stress you're under? It sure did help me and I'm certain it will do the same for you.

What is your industry looking for in an applicant

The next right step in discovering *your* best career option(s) is to know what your industry is looking for. For example, if you have a degree in business and have decided you want to focus on jobs in the banking industry, you need to find out where the greatest hiring potential is *within* the banking industry. Is it compliance? Human resources? Operations and management? Once you know where the most need is, you will know how to proceed in presenting yourself— which elements of your experience and education to highlight.

Decide where you want to start and why

You also need to determine where and how you want to or are willing to enter your career field.

- Do you want to start at the ground level of a large company and work your way up over time?
- Do you want to take an entry or mid-level position with a large company in order to have the prestige of working there on your resume so you can get to a higher level position with a smaller company in less time?
- Do you want to start small, as in a small company, get a few years of experience under your belt, and then move up to a larger company?
- Do you want to work for a small to mid-level company and

settle in; working your way up to the top, having a history with the company, and it being 'like family'?

Do you see where this is going? You need to have an idea of what your overall goals are—not job goals, per se, but *professional* goals. In other words, how corporate-like do you want to be? Do you want a fast-paced environment where things are always changing and the challenges are non-stop? Or do you want a slower-paced more people-oriented environment? Do you want your focus to be on the business of doing business or do you want to be in the business of helping people take care of their business matters?

Knowing, or at least having an idea of these things, serves to get you on the right career path for you.

How

Much of the 'how' in getting these things done has to come from you. You have to **decide** to follow the steps I've given you. You have to **decide** to work from the answers you obtain from the questions you have asked yourself.

It is the 'working from the answers' that brings others into the equation. Once you know (or at least have a relatively good idea) which direction you want to take your career and where you want to begin, it is time to do a bit of research and networking—two very important elements in establishing and maintaining a happy and successful life (career-wise and otherwise).

Here's how to research the companies you might want to work for:

Find out who the employers are in your field

- Large, small, in-between; make a list of potential employers within the geographical area you are willing to live and work.

You can use the internet, your college career counselors and website, family, friends, and even products. For example, an author friend of mine was asked by someone wanting to publish their first children's book, how to find a publisher. My friends reply was this, "Go to a book store and your local library. Look for books that are along the same lines as your book in regards to the intended audience and formatting. When you find them, look inside the book and see who the publisher is. Make a list of these publishers and then contact them. Don't go for the big name publishers. They won't talk to you. Look for the smaller publishing houses."

- Remember to think outside the box EXAMPLE: Lawyers don't have to work for a law firm. Large companies often hire in-house lawyers

Study their website—particularly their mission statements, their history, and their company overview

- How long have they been in business
- Do they offer services or goods you are interested in working with and representing
- Do they seem progressive—willing to adapt to necessary changes, or are they building their business and their reputation on being stalwart and committed to the original product or service (both have their merits)

Research the company's reputation, principles, and integrity

- Google prospective employers to find out about complaints, litigations, their reputation, etc. Make sure, however, that you verify information by following through on outcome of complaints and so forth. NOTE: You can be sure they will do the same with you, should you apply
- LINKEDIN (www.linkedin.com) is a wonderful source for checking out the company's management team and employees. Simply do a name search and see what comes up.
- Glassdoor is a valuable and reputable site for doing company research: https://www.glassdoor.com/Reviews/index.htm

Talk to job recruiters from the company.

Talk to friends, family, and fellow-alum who have worked for or who have done business with the companies you are considering.

- What do they have to say about the company?

- Does what you learn sound like a good fit for your skills and personality?

Visit the company as a potential customer/client. A lot can be learned about a business just by walking through the door.

- Are they friendly?
- Is the place clean and pleasant-looking?
- Is there palpable tension between employees or do they seem at ease and comfortable with each other?
- Do their actions and attitudes match up with the way they represent themselves online and through advertising?
- Can you see yourself spending hours a day there five days a week…and feeling good about yourself in doing so?
- If you have the opportunity to visit on a regular basis, do you notice much turn-over in the employees?

Study their employment policies and openings (from their website and sites like Glassdoor).

- Do they offer competitive salaries and benefits?
- Are they even hiring? What is their turn-over rate?
- What type of attitude do they take toward family?

It is important that you have a basic knowledge of these things prior to applying for a position. Doing so saves you and the company time and energy if you aren't a good match.

Here's how to network with potential employers:

- **Job shadow.** Not only will this help get your foot in the door, it will give you a bird's eye look at what you would be doing and possibly help you decide which direction you want your career to take.

- **Get involved in your community.** Community involvement and participation in fundraising events and such is a wonderful way to meet business owners/managers and to let them see your skills and personality in action.

- **Join a civic group.** A local civic group like the Lion's Club, Jaycees, Optimist Club, etc. helps develop relationships which can lead to gainful employment. It is important, however, that you aren't doing these things simply for that reason. It will show and will be a major red flag and turnoff to the very ones you want to impress.

- **Follow and comment on their Twitter account (if they have one).** Same goes for their Facebook page. But be sure you don't post or tweet anything negative on their sites OR yours. They will undoubtedly check you out, which is what you want…as long as you give them something positive to see/read when they do.

- **Join LinkedIn and request potential employers to add you to their contact list.** Post comments about your job experience and career goals on your page so they can be seen. 'Like' theirs, as well. EXAMPLE: This book is an excellent example of how well LinkedIn works. In writing this book I realized I needed another set of eyes to edit and to act as an advisor and sounding board. Through LinkedIn (I promise I'm not being paid to promote them. It's just a really great resource ☺) I 'met' the person who has served in those capacities for me. Our career paths, our backgrounds, even the generations we come from are complete polar opposites, but we were an instant mesh when it comes to working together. Our paths, however, would have never crossed had it not been for the networking available through this site, so it speaks for itself.

- **Ask friends and family members for introductions.** You need to exercise a great deal of care and caution with this, though, and here's why: The friendships and working relationships between your friends and family members and the people you want to connect can become strained if you don't meet their expectations, if you misrepresent yourself, or if you fail to fulfill your commitment to a job. Steve is the not-so-perfect perfect example of what I'm talking about…

Without his brother in-law's permission (or even notifying him afterwards), Steve used his brother in-law as a reference on a job application for position with the state police. The brother in-law, you see, works as a state police officer and is highly respected within the organization.

Steve was granted an interview but when he was nearly thirty minutes late and the interviewer couldn't reach him by phone, the interviewer called Steve's brother in-law to see if he knew why he hadn't shown up yet. Completely unaware of what was going on or that his name had been given as a reference, the brother in-law told his superior officer that he knew nothing about it, that Steve's behavior was very typical for him, and that he hoped this would in no way adversely affect *his* (the officer's) reputation or relationship with his superiors or within the organization as a whole.

The interviewer assured him all was well—that his record and integrity spoke for itself. As for Steve, he never showed up. Never called. Nothing. He was simply too lazy or scared to face the interviewer because he knew he was not qualified for the position. You can also probably guess it did nothing positive for the relationship between him and his sister and brother in-law.

On a much brighter note, however, several years ago, a middle-aged friend of mine wanted to do the work-school program for her senior year in high school. She and her boyfriend planned to get married shortly after graduation (which wasn't all that uncommon then), so she wanted to get a head start on a good job. After giving it some thought, Darcy decided she would like to work in a bank. Her dad talked to the president and vice-president of the bank his insurance company did business with. They were completely sold on the idea of participating in the cooperative education program with the school, so they offered Darcy a job—even saying she could work full-time that summer before school started if she wanted to.

Darcy jumped on the opportunity; loving everything about the job. And they 'loved' her right back. Darcy worked for the bank for five years—right up until the day before she and her husband moved from the area in order for him to accept a promotion for his job and only weeks before she gave birth to their first child.

Thirty-five years later Darcy and her former boss and his wife still exchange Christmas cards and periodic letters throughout the year and Darcy still gets together with two of the 'girls' she worked with during that time.

See? It can work. Just be sure you do your part to make it work the right way.

- Internships are a great way to connect if you are still in school.
- Submit a resume (if appropriate). This really is considered a step beyond networking. Call it intense-networking, if you want to. Submitting a resume sends the message that you are serious about your desire to work for a company or organization, so please make sure you are—or as certain as you can be, anyway*—before you do.

*Remember: Your first job will not likely be your last and your first place of employment will not likely be your only place of employment throughout your career. We millennials aren't like that (for the most part). And that's okay. Just be sure that when you accept a position, you will give 100% of your skills, your integrity, and your desire to be the best possible employee you can be while you are there.

Chapter 5

Personal Branding

Take a look at the logos above. Did you immediately recognize all of them? If you use any of the products these logos represent, why do you use them? What messages do these logos convey to you?

A logo carries a heavy load of responsibility. It is the job of the logo to draw people in—to create an appeal, to build consumer trust, and to generate instant recognition in the minds of consumers. Logos are promises of value.

In other words, even though we say a book can't be judged by its cover, that's exactly what a logo is trying to accomplish. Business and product marketing professionals want us to become so logo-minded that we equate the logo with the quality, desirability, and usefulness of a product. For example, the Dunkin' Donuts (DD) logo uses a font that closely resembles the springy, soft, roundness of a donut, while the color choices promote a cheery, care-free attitude.

When developing a brand and brand logo, marketing and product development professionals put a considerable amount of time and energy into designing a logo that:

- **Is visually appealing and evokes the proper emotions for the product or service being sold**. Examples: For fresh food labels, some shades of green work well, but in others, green tends to make consumers think of mold, so it should be avoided. Blue, on the other hand, instills confidence and trust. It makes us feel comfortable and safe and 'says' that the service or product has integrity.
- **Is memorable**. Brand developers want you to see the logo and know it belongs to their service or product. They also want the logo to be prominent so that you recognize their service or product on the shelves, in an ad, or on a sign while driving down the road, quicker than you recognize anyone else's.

Now let's look at branding from the consumer's point of view.

We choose the brands we choose for a variety of reasons. Sometimes we choose brands based on advertising and/or peer pressure. Sometimes we choose brands because we may have an emotional connection to it: Your mom always used that laundry soap, your first pair of soccer cleats were that brand. You ate that brand of peanut butter every day for lunch as a kid.

Regardless of your reasons for choosing one particular brand over another, whether you realize it or not, you ask yourself the following questions when making those choices: What is it that draws you to a particular brand? What makes you loyal to one brand over another? Does it meet your expectations? Does it exceed your expectations? Does it produce consistent results?

The answers to those questions (as well as a few more) determine the choices and decisions you make as a consumer. In other words, proper branding is an indispensable and crucial element when it comes to the success (or lack of) of a service or product. But products and services aren't the only things these branding questions apply to. They also apply to you and your professional life.

YOU are a product/service in need of branding

Building your reputation and level of recognition in your field of expertise requires you to market yourself. And in order to do so with optimal success, you need to build your own personal brand.

Your personal brand represents how you see yourself as well as how others see you. Your personal brand advertises or publicizes:

- Your personal and professional image and reputation
- The professional qualities and attributes that set you apart and cause you to rise above others

Do you see the parallels between traditional branding in the sense we think of it and your personal branding? Just like any other product or service manufacturer out there, you want to grab and hold on to peoples' attention, let them know you are able to produce results that meet or exceed their expectations, and that are consistent and reliable.

What your brand needs to convey

There are several characteristics of a successful brand—the most important being consistency, visibility, originality, and fit.

Visibility:

- Are you visible to or findable by your target market? Do the employers you want to connect with know that you exist?

Michelle works fulltime as the supervisor of admissions at the hospital in her community. She enjoys the people she works with and the job isn't mind-numbing, but Michelle is extremely creative and an excellent seamstress. Ever since her grandmother taught her how to sew before she was even a teenager, Michelle has been turning out amazing quilts, doll clothes for her daughter and her daughter's friends, intricate baby items, and clothing for herself and others. She is *amazingly* talented.

On more than one occasion she has been asked why she doesn't do more with her talent, as in selling her items in stores and online. When asked, Michelle smiles shyly, shrugs her shoulders, and says, "That would be great, but I wouldn't know where to start."

Most people's reply to Michelle is something like, "You're missing out because you could sell things faster than you could make them." Or, "Just get on Etsy or Facebook and start selling. Your stuff is great!" But Michelle's tendency to be a bit under-confident or too humble, kept her from doing anything.

A little over two years ago, though, Michelle's daughter decided to help her mom out by using her mom's talents to 'start' a business for a class project in school. Taking the project a few steps farther than required, Michelle's daughter put together a very basic and rudimentary business plan that included marketing and pricing and profit vs. cost projections. After making sure her mom wouldn't go nuts on her, she then posted some pictures on her social media and a few other sites (including setting up an Etsy store). She also started making an effort to let her peers know when she was wearing or carrying a bag her mom had made. Within three days, orders started coming in from the girls at school and people all across the country who saw the pictures online.

Today Michelle works fewer hours at the hospital—just enough to keep her benefits—and is enjoying her new and very profitable home business—one she says doesn't really seem like work because she truly loves what she's doing. People all across the country are wearing or using something Michelle made.

Michelle was always talented and capable of doing what she does. But it wasn't until she made herself **visible** that her unique talents started speaking for themselves.

So when you think about how branding yourself, you need to ask:

- Are you putting yourself out there so people will know you are there and what you have to offer?
- Are you attending networking events to begin building those relationships with professionals and potential employers?
- Are you using and exhibiting your skills and knowledge in places and ways that they can be seen and appreciated?
- Are you portraying yourself appropriately and favorably?

Consistency:

It is important…even essential, to make an effort to communicate your unique value that sets you apart (favorably) from others in your field in every forum and interaction. This aspect of your branding is what tells people you are ready, willing, and able to consistently produce the quality of work and results they are looking for. This happens when you:

- Have proof to back up what you say you can do. EXAMPLE: If you portray yourself as a strong leader, you need to be able to prove you have leadership experience. Just 'knowing' you can do it isn't enough for most prospective employers when looking for someone to lead a team, project, or branch of their business.

The consistency of your brand also needs to 'paint' you in a consistent light. So ask yourself:

- Is your brand consistently promoting the same 'results' and information? In other words, do your application documents (application, resume, cover letter, etc.) and communication (in person, email, and social media) represent the same information?
- Are you highlighting your brand in a professional manner regardless of who you are connecting with? EXAMPLE: Is your social media portraying what you want your brand to portray? It's all out there and it's all going to be scrutinized by prospective employers and associates, so you need to be very aware of this.

The infamous outlet malls we all (or most of us, anyway) love to shop at are another example of brand consistency.

The labels on the clothes denote designer and high-end; causing people to grab them up at what they believe to be bargain prices because of the long-standing *visibility* and *consistency* that resonates with consumers when they see their logos. But the truth of the matter is that the vast majority of the time, the merchandise sold in these settings is made for these brands specifically for sale in these settings. And as for the bargain you are getting…it's just a suggestion of what it might bring. By and large consumers are satisfied with the quality of outlet mall merchandise. Even if it isn't the 'real thing', most agree that a lower-end product by a high-end brand is better than one from a low-end brand.

That's okay for clothing, purses, and sunglasses, but it's not okay for you. There's only one of you. So you have to make certain that your consistency is…consistent. If you want to capture and hold the attention and respect of people in your field you have to take every opportunity to say who you are and always be who you say you are.

Originality:

You have to be deliberate in communicating what you want to be known for and how you want to be viewed. Much like consistency, originality in branding is meant to make you stand out from the crowd (in a good way). So when thinking about your personal branding in terms of originality, you need to ask yourself:

- How are you going to make your experience, skills, and qualifications stand out over your competitors? And how are you going to do this without coming off as arrogant and prideful? How can you build yourself up without tearing others down?
- What should your audience remember most about you?
- What do you want to be known for on a professional level? EXAMPLE: Do you want to focus on the fact that you are an innovative up and coming professional who has knowledge and training in the latest advancements in your field, or do you want to focus on the fact that you have a solid track record for making sure the little details that often get missed, don't?
- What kind of person do you want people to know you are? EXAMPLE: Do you want to be described by interviewers as driven, innovative, and 'going places', or as solid, methodical, and detail-oriented?

A lot of how you present yourself in the area of originality will depend on your chosen field. There's not a lot of wiggle room for innovation and creativity when it comes to professions like patent law or insurance claims adjusting, but teaching and factory production managers have the opportunity to use their originality to enhance their productivity and output results, thus greatly raising their level of desirability.

Fit:

When thinking of how you are going to brand yourself, you need to make sure that the image and message you send fits the needs and desires of the people and businesses you want to attract.

- How are you going to show that you are a good fit for the company?
- Would you represent the industry/company well?
- Are the qualities you are marketing what your perspective employers are looking for?
- What pertinent jobs or skills have you had that demonstrate your ability to contribute to the company/organization?
- Do you have the personality and temperament that will reflect the image and message the company/organization wants to reflect?

In looking for examples of what does and doesn't work when it comes to branding, I came across a website containing some major faux paus solid companies made in regards to their fit in cultures and people groups outside their normal sphere of influence. For the most part these companies and businesses have their act together, but for whatever reason, they missed the boat when it came time to brand themselves in certain places.

Below is a partial list—the ones I found to be most humorous and/or most costly. Take a look for yourself. But while you're laughing, remember that you, too, need to be careful of not doing the very same thing to yourself.

- Clairol launched a curling iron called "Mist Stick" in Germany even though "mist" is German slang for manure.
- Coca-Cola's brand name, when first marketed in China, was sometimes translated as "Bite The Wax Tadpole."
- Colgate launched toothpaste in France named "Cue" without realizing that it's also the name of a French pornographic magazine.
- Ford blundered when marketing the Pinto in Brazil because the term in Brazilian Portuguese means "tiny male genitals."
- Ikea products were marketed in Thailand with Swedish names that in the Thai language mean "sex" and "getting to third base."

How do you build your personal brand

There is no instant branding package available. You have to start from scratch. Remember…this is YOUR brand so it needs to be *about* you and created *by* you. But since you know yourself better than anyone else does, it really isn't all that hard to do.

Step one: Identify your:

- **Strengths:** What do you do best? What are your pride points? What areas of knowledge and skills are you most confident about?
- **Unique Values:** What do you believe in; both personal and professional? Values are tricky. On one hand, you want to find a job that is comparable to all, or most of your values. On the other hand, it is important for you to know that a single work environment may not be able to fulfill your ideal work environment or agree with you on all of your personal values. So while you definitely need to make them part of your brand, you need to be prepared to make a few

compromises early-on in your career. But before you do, you need to know how much you are willing to compromise. There are some jobs, no matter how lucrative or prestigious they are, that aren't worth the amount of compromise it would require some people to make. It is also important for you to remember that your first job may not be as "glamourous" as you are expecting. So don't let your sense of identity and branding make you too proud or too arrogant to get your foot in the door of your chosen field or industry, but don't sell out just for a job. Find that balance—the one you can live with and still maintain your identity (brand), and go with it.

- **Attributes:** How would others describe you? How would you describe yourself? Don't be afraid or embarrassed to ask someone to help you on this one. And don't be insulted or defensive about the answers you get.
- **Qualifications:** Remember that you have these. You have a degree, certification, and/or license. You have applicable skills. Remember to include those transferrable skills that many employers look for, such as communication, leadership, time-management bi-lingual capabilities, networking connections and so forth. Provide examples of how you have demonstrated these skills in the past and any relevant results they produced.
- **Passions:** What drives you? What excites you? What motivates you? Make sure your passion is shown through your conversations and on paper.

REMEMBER: Just like the products we pull from the shelves, people make decisions about us based on our brands. They will decide if they want to establish a relationship with us or connect us with opportunities based on our personal branding.

How do you communicate (advertise) your brand

Marketing message:

This is your formal introduction of yourself. Think of this as your magazine ad, your billboard, your television commercial, or your popup ad on the sidebar of an email account.

The main purpose of your marketing message is to promote your brand (YOU). You do this by making sure the first impression or exposure someone has to you reflects the following:

- Education
- Related Skills
- Areas of Expertise
- Personal Characteristics
- Accomplishments
- Career Focus: What information are you looking for? Hint… Avoid saying, I am looking for a job. Instead, communicate your interest in learning more about them and their business. Remember, just like a brand, when people like you they will invest in you.

What does this message look like

Your marketing message will have various forms—just like any other product. More specifically you need to have both a formal and informal marketing message.

The Formal Message should be a 30-45 second message. Most people will call this your 'elevator speech'—short enough to give in the time it takes to make it between floors on an elevator and packed with enough information to make an impression.

The Informal Message is more conversational. This is what you share with friends, family, or close acquaintances.

REMEMBER: Your marketing message should be tailored. It should be relevant to the person that you are communicating with. Remember, though, your goal isn't to tell your life story. Your goal is to keep it specific to your academic and professional background. You are selling yourself professionally…not signing up for an online dating site.

You also need to remember to make sure your brand message is relevant and precisely tailored to pique the interest of the person you are speaking to or communicating with. Make sure you do your RESEARCH. Research the person, their industry, background, and any other available information that will give you an idea of who they are and what they are looking for in an employee or business partner.

HINT: Sites such as LinkedIn are very helpful in doing that.

Branding is essential for success

Even if you didn't previously think of it as branding, selling yourself, as in going after the position you want and taking your career to the next level, is just that. And it happens best when you follow the guidelines marketing professionals follow when marketing goods or services to consumers:

- Be visible
- Be consistent
- Be original
- Make sure your message fits

NOTE: To help you on your way to creating and developing your personal brand, complete the exercise on the following pages.

Use the space below to begin outlining a marketing message that you hope to deliver to someone in your field:

Education

Related Skills

Areas of Expertise

Personal Characteristics

Accomplishments

Career Focus

TIPS:

- Reassess your personal brand regularly to see if you are representing yourself in a way that is relevant and marketable. (Friends and mentors are very helpful in this process)

- Damaged brands are very hard to repair. A brand is like a GPA: It can be hard to build, but very easy to bring down.

Chapter 6:

Networking

Networking is a powerful word describing a powerful and essential concept. The fact that networking is so important makes it something many find intimidating…even scary. I get that. Because even though I've understood the importance of networking since my earliest days in college, I've struggled with feeling confident about my networking abilities. I never really felt I was very effective—that I was doing it 'right'. But my biggest concern, I have to admit, was the fear of rejection or being ignored. No one likes rejection, right? So why put myself out there as a target, I thought? And so I didn't.

I avoided networking because I didn't understand this simple truth: Networking isn't a sales pitch (you're not selling you). Networking is about getting to know other people and letting them get to know you…on a professional level, of course. The purpose is to make connections that can (and hopefully will) lead to:

- Future clients
- Future employment opportunities
- Future resources for doing your job better
- Resources that will allow you to better showcase your talents and abilities; bringing you new and exciting possibilities
- Resources for partnering on projects that can impact the community as well as your professional life (and theirs, too)
- Creating a reputation for yourself in the business world—you will be a name and face people will recognize and want to call on
- Relationships that can serve as professional mentors

I don't see anything on that list about handing out copies of your resume like they are candy on Halloween, do you? I'll say it again…networking is meant to establish and build relationships *so that when someone with your qualifications is needed, YOU will be the first person that comes to mind.* So when it comes to networking, the best advice I can give you about networking is this: Do it. Do lots of it, but don't let your previous misconceptions about networking pull you in the wrong direction. You have a voice and a brand that deserves to be seen, heard and represented, so let networking fulfill its true purpose and start making a name and reputation for yourself the right way.

The elements of successful networking

Now that you know what networking *really* is (establishing and building business-related relationships with others), let's take a look at the three basic elements of networking and how make them work for you…

ESTABLISH: I remember serving on a discussion panel a few years ago on the topic of networking. One of the panelists said, "Networking is not just about who you know, but who knows you." And he was right—networking is a two-way street. Give and take. It's just like friendship—only on a professional level instead of a personal one. So to help you understand the element of establishing a network of relationships, think about your best friend and/or your partner. How did you meet? After that initial introduction, what information was shared that caused a deeper friendship to form? No one forced you to become friends. It happened because of that initial introduction, followed by conversations revealing shared interests and so forth. In a word, these relationships are genuine.

The same must be said about your networking relationships. There has to be an initial introduction, followed by conversation during which you briefly and concisely share your skills, goals, and professional aspirations (short and long term) *as well as* learning the same from the person you are talking to. These conversations also need to make both of you privy to ways you can use (in a good way) one another as a resource for getting from Point A to Point B in your career plan, enhance your skills, and/or help you create more favorable presence in your community.

A great example of how this works can be seen in the following:

Deanna has spent years in youth and family ministry. She spends a major part of summer working as a mentor at a summer camp. One evening, some of the former campers came to visit—young adults Deanna had spent summer after summer with. As Deanna was visiting with them, one of them, a young woman by the name of Chelsea, mentioned that she was strongly considering a master's program at a university near where Deanna lived. She was expressing the desire to find a suitable roommate to share living expenses with and asked Deanna if she knew of anyone. Deanna didn't, but said she would ask around to see if she could find someone.

Less than a week later, Deanna received an email from the niece of one of her dearest friends. This young woman told Deanna she needed the very same thing Chelsea needed—a suitable roommate to share living expenses with while she, too, was completing her master's program at the very same university.

Both Chelsea and the other young woman were networking; reaching out to someone who was in a position to possibly help them come up with a solution to their situation. Neither girl knew the other, but because of their networking, Deanna was able to connect the two of them together and now they are living together and pursuing their educational and professional goals.

See how that works? Pretty cool, huh?

BUILDING: Do you typically declare someone to be your best friend after one conversation? Or even two? No, friendships are built over time—time spent talking, doing things together, and learning to respect and appreciate each other. Oh, and one more thing…friendships require mutual effort. You can't be BFFs with someone you don't know or who won't talk to you.

The same holds true for networking. To consider someone a professional contact requires more than meeting with them once and exchanging pleasantries or even having a conversation over coffee or while waiting for a meeting to start. For example, let's say you attend a career fair or professional event where there are going to be several potential employers in attendance. You introduce yourself. That's called an initial connection. But I think you will agree an introduction such as this hardly constitutes a relationship. No, a relationship would begin to form if you spent a few minutes talking, exchanged contact information, *and then* actually followed through on *reconnecting* again and again. But remember: just like friendships, building professional relationships requires mutual effort.

To help you fully understand what I'm saying, let's look at a few examples of what this looks like…

Mark met several HR people at a career fair sponsored by the university. There were two individuals that really made a positive impression on him. Not only did he like them, but he was very impressed with the companies they represented. But meeting them was all he did; saying hello, shaking their hand, taking their card, and spending a couple of minutes reading the table display. He *did* take the time to ask one of the men a question; one he hoped sounded intelligent and proved his interest in the company, but he never made mention of being interested in a particular job or saying anything to the man as to why he (Mark) would be a good fit for the company.

A couple of weeks after the event, however, he called both men to 'touch base' and request an interview. Both men, however, had no recollection of Mark. One even went so far as to say, "After the first hour or so, all you kids look the same to me. I don't remember anyone who doesn't take the time and effort to make themselves unforgettable."

This wasn't networking. In fact, it is the perfect example of what NOT to do.

Katy attended the same job fair as Mark. She, too, made contact with a few reps with companies she was interested in working for. One in particular, was a company based out of a town she'd visited often—the town her grandparents lived in. After introducing herself, Katy briefly shared two or three memories of the town; saying she would feel confident in putting down roots there.

That single comment opened the door for a little more conversation and made a lasting impression on the company's representative. Before Katy moved on, she was given a business card with a phone number to the representatives' direct line and instructions to contact his secretary to set up a tour of the company. Katy accepted the invitation and two weeks after taking the tour, she was offered a job. Five years later she is still there and is training to take over the job of the man she met at the job fair that day (he's retiring).

Katy didn't 'brown nose' or try to sell herself during that initial introduction. She initiated a business-level friendship by finding common ground and shared interests. These things then led to an invitation to take things to the next level and then on to the level of a professional working relationship.

That is networking.

Elizabeth and John are farmers—not something most of us millennials think about, but Elizabeth's 'networking story' is one worth sharing because it shows just how significant the seemingly-insignificant things can be…

Elizabeth and John were representing their state's sheep at an agricultural show one Saturday when Elizabeth decided to walk around and see some of the other displays and do a bit of networking. A sign in front of a tent announcing a seminar for something called 'value-added agriculture'. Elizabeth didn't have a clue as to what that was, but she decided to find out. Thirty minutes later she left the tent full of ideas to diversify their operation. And did she ever!

Elizabeth will tell you to this day (some fifteen years later) that thirty minutes changed her life; opening doors she previously didn't even know existed and tripling the income of their farm in less than two years.

While I won't go into the details of Elizabeth's value-added business ventures, I will say that the degree of success is largely dependent on establishing and maintaining a variety of business relationships that are 'outside the box' of the traditional agricultural 'world'. In other words…networking.

So remember, while networking isn't about friendships, per se, it *is* about relationships. In order for networking to be legit, there has to be a relationship of the business kind. There needs to be a mutual effort to converse and communicate. There needs to be a familiarity that goes beyond recognizing and acknowledging each other in public with a polite nod and greeting. So once the introductions have taken place and a relationship is established, you need to do your part to maintain the relationship so that it will be both useful and beneficial.

MAINTAINING: Think of a friend that you have lost touch with over the course of your life. Maybe they moved away. Maybe you did. Maybe your circumstances changed—marriage, divorce, new interests…regardless of the reason, friendships transition and even end all the time. Why? A lack of maintenance (maintaining), that's why.

School—especially grade and high school—is the perfect example of this. How many kids in grade school did you pinky-swear or make a pact with to be bff's with…*forever*? How many guys on the team are you still in touch with? How many of your fellow-cheerleaders or drama team cohorts do you still talk to on a regular basis? Is your first one and only true love *still* your one and only true love?

We didn't expect (or want) the relationship to end. We didn't purposely lie to one another, but let's face it—when your best friend moves six states away, it's not easy to stay best friends. Even with all the technological benefits we have today to help us stay in touch with one another, Facebook messages just aren't the same as being able to have a face-to-face conversation or work through your frustration by hitting a few balls or shooting hoops with someone you can trust to listen and give you sound advice.

And then there are those unfortunate events that lead to the end of a relationship. Gossip, peer pressure, and simply outgrowing each other play a role in 'relationships gone bad' at one time or another in everyone's life. We don't like it, but it happens. Most of us would agree, however, that we don't let these events destroy us or hold us hostage. No, we move forward. On to bigger and better things, right?

But networking isn't about making friendships (on a purely social level), you say? So why bring up all these thoughts and memories about the girls who turned on me, the guy who ratted me out, or the girl/guy that broke my heart? Because the same rules that apply to these types of relationships apply to the rules of networking, that's why. And here's another thing…there are times when the two (personal friendships and business relationships) actually do cross paths.

Here are a few examples (both good and not-so-good) of this 'double-sided relationship'…

CASE #1-Succesful friend/business relationship crossover:

Gene and Ben grew up in the same small, rural town. The boys played and went to school together until Ben and his family moved thirty miles away during the boys' sophomore year in high school. This was long before the days of cellphones and the internet, and we all 'know' it's not 'cool' for boys to write letters, so they basically lost touch with one another.

Fast-forward seven years. Following in his brothers' footsteps, Ben served four years in the Army following his graduation from high school and then used his GI Bill (government college fund) to go to school at a small university less than a hundred miles from home. One day while walking downtown, Ben ran into Gene. As it turned out, Gene and his new bride, along with Gene's parents had moved there and had opened an insurance business.

In the course of their conversation Ben told Gene he would soon graduate with a degree in accounting and was soon to be married. They exchanged phone numbers and promises to get together again soon. That evening Ben received a phone call from Gene's dad, Joe—a man Ben had grown up knowing, liking, and respecting. Joe offered Ben a job on the spot as the accountant for their new company. He could finish his schooling and work at the same time.

Ben accepted the job, brought his new bride to town a few months later, and retired from the highly successful company after forty-five years of dedicated service. Oh, and he and Gene are still the best of friends.

This is an obvious case of networking with friends that turned out great.

CASE #2-Business relationships that turn into friendships:

The summer before her senior year in high school, Marley went to work as a teller at the bank her mom worked for. It was part of a work-study program through her school. The job continued into the school year and the following summer after she graduated.

Marley enjoyed the work and the customers she met. Marley's customers liked her too. So did Marley's boss—so much so that she offered Marley a part-time job when she started college. Marley planned to attend a local college, so keeping her job allowed her to have the best of both worlds. But at the time, not even she knew just what an impact this would have on her life.

Two weeks into her first semester of college, the bank hired another part-time teller. He was chosen for the job after Marley and her boss had talked with him at a hiring event for college students like herself. He had impressed both Marley and her boss with his easy-going confidence that wasn't cocky or arrogant. It was obvious he was just being himself and they both felt he would fit in well with the other tellers. And they were right. Brad was easy and fun to work with. He was professional, yet had a great sense of humor that put a smile on the face of his customers and co-workers. Marley also admitted to her girlfriends that Brad wasn't bad to look at, either.

Apparently, the feeling was mutual, because a couple of months after the two started working together, Brad asked Marley on a date—a Halloween costume party. From that evening on, Brad and Marley were a couple. A little over a year later, they were married. Because both were well-loved and respected by their co-workers and bosses, they were allowed to continue working at the bank together while they finished school.

Everyone was sad to see Brad and Marley go when they quit their jobs to relocate after graduating; Marley with a degree in marketing and Brad with a degree in banking and finance. Brad is now working for another small-town bank as a vice president and is still the warm, personable guy he's always been. "He's great for business," his boss readily tells everyone. Marley works for the state's tourism division developing unique and innovative programs and venues to get people into the state's parks, museums, and other historical sites.

Networking with her boss resulted in Marley gaining a co-worker, friend, and husband. I'd say that was three hours standing behind a table on campus well spent. Wouldn't you?

CASE #3-Friends and business don't always mix:

Lauren and Rebecca had been friends in high school. Close friends. But like most of us, they drifted apart during college. But when the two met up at their five-year class reunion, they discovered they both had a passion for all things vintage and antique. As they talked, they realized they shared several business contacts and that their goals for starting their own business were quite similar. They also discovered they lived within twenty miles of each other. One thing led to another and six months after the reunion Lauren and Rebecca decided to go into business together. Laruen had the better head for business, so that would be her focus, and Rebecca, being the more creative one, would handle the bulk of the marketing. Together they would mesh their styles of refurbishing, refinishing, and repurposing to create a distinct style they were sure would set them apart for all the rest.

Things went well for the first three years. So well, in fact, that their business caught the eye of some really big names (I can't list them here for privacy purposes). So when Lauren suggested they relocate to a suburban area closer to either Chicago or Dallas, she assumed Rebecca would be all in. Not. So. Much. Rebecca 'argued' that in living close to a large city she wouldn't have nearly as much potential for finding bargains at estate sales and yard sales. She would feel pressured to produce and she just didn't like the idea.

They went back and forth for several months; talking to people they trusted and to one another. When no resolution was reached, Lauren decided she was going out on her own. She wanted to go where the big money was and the better opportunities for exposure. This hurt Rebecca deeply and the two parted the company with hurt feelings and resentment toward one another.

Neither Lauren nor Rebecca is enjoying their work the way they used to nor enjoying the same degree of success as they did when they were together.

In this case, networking brought friends back together as friends and business partners. But in the end, both the friendship and the business fell apart.

It's not easy

One could easily argue that maintaining a relationship is the most difficult part of networking. It's somewhat easy to shake a hand, say hello, and introduce yourself (even for those of you who are shy or feel like a fish out of water in a group larger than three). Even making a follow-up contact or two isn't all that taxing. But the art of effective networking is perfected by *maintaining* the contacts you have made and turned into budding relationships *so that they become bona fide* relationships.

Again, networking is not a one-time effort. Networking has to include follow-up, persistence and consistency in order to be bona fide networking.

- Following up just for the sake of keeping in touch and making sure the contact person remembers your name is vital.
- Keeping your networking contacts updated on new projects or professional experiences is also important. Just like your situations and needs change, so do theirs.

- Failure to maintain a professional networking connection could present challenges in your job search. Being recognized and remembered by a potential employer puts you in a much healthier position than having to remind that same potential employer that the two of you met…that one time…at a job fair…three years ago.
- Maintaining contact with networking contacts every few months or maybe even a work anniversary is fine. Just prior to and soon after an annual meeting or conference you both attend is also smart.

Okay, so now that you know what networking is (and isn't), let's move on to how you get the job done.

Effective networking strategies

Above all else, effective networking must be **genuine**. No one likes a phony. It is demeaning. When you try to schmooze someone, you are essentially telling them they are ignorant in regard to reading people. You are saying they aren't intelligent enough or worthy of seeing and knowing the real you. In short, being anything less than genuine and sincere is insulting.

If, however, you express genuine interest and respect for someone's time, position, intellect, and knowledge of the trade, you are a) giving that person what they deserve and b) you are sending the message that you will do the same for their company.

What's more, by being genuine you are putting your true assets and capabilities on display. Your genuineness is the part of networking that 'sells you' to someone.

And finally, a genuine attitude makes it easier for you to remember your contacts and what you need to know about them. By being genuine your head isn't filled with the junk of trying to keep up a façade.

Along with being genuine, it is essential that you be **truthful**. Sooner or later the truth always comes out, and from a professional standpoint, you ALWAYS want to tell the truth, the whole truth, and nothing but the truth. Lying about your abilities and accomplishments is professional suicide!

Twenty-something Matthew is a young man of integrity. He wouldn't lie about anything—especially his work. So when he caught a co-worker falsifying reports (while doing his normal job), he brought it to the attention of his boss. Months went by and nothing was done. After a year went by and still nothing was done to stop the deceit (and theft), Matthew decided to leave the company.

Within forty-eight hours of posting his resume online, he received nearly thirty hits and four phone calls requesting him to come for an interview. The company Matthew chose to work for was hiring for two positions—his and one filled by someone with supposedly similar qualifications and supposedly a few more years of experience.

While the company itself is one of integrity, it soon became apparent to Matthew and his superiors that the other new employee had embellished his resume (to say the least). He had used the professional networking sites to gain a position he wasn't qualified to fill. This man's untruthfulness got him the job, but it certainly didn't allow him to keep the job. Less than a month after being hired, he was fired for inability to perform his duties and for misrepresenting himself.

"Doesn't anyone tell the truth?" Matthew asked. "Don't they realize that at some point they are going to have to back up what they say?"

You also have to be **accessible**. You cannot expect to meet people and develop a network of business contacts if you don't put yourself out there. You don't have to be the proverbial life of the party or be the kind of person that never meets a stranger or forgets a name, but you DO have to make the effort to be where you can meet people and they can meet you.

Here are some of the ways you can and should make yourself accessible:

Company picnics and holiday parties. Your presence gives you the ability to get to know your coworkers and superiors on a different level than just that of the office. Your attendance provides insight to what their hobbies and outside interests are, their family, and their personality. Knowing these things gives you 'connect points'; things to talk about and ways to possibly let your abilities and character shine.

Eric and Susan attend the Christmas party and summer picnic given by Eric's workplace every year. It's not something they would call the highlights of their year, but they know it is the right thing to do. A couple of years ago, however, attending the picnic turned into a great opportunity for their daughter, who had just obtained her teaching degree.

Eric, who is a department manager, introduced Susan to Grant, who had just recently joined the company as head of another department. Grant introduced both Eric and Susan to his wife, Leann, who they discovered was the new principal at the junior high school in a small town about ten miles away. During the course of the conversation, Susan was able to share that their daughter had just obtained her teaching certificate. Leann expressed interest in having the young woman contact her about a job. The seventh-grade English teacher had to resign unexpectedly to care for her husband who had been diagnosed with cancer.

While this situation was definitely sad and unfortunate, the fact that both men took the time and effort to network resulted in Susan and Leann connecting, which led to a job for Eric and Susan's daughter and resolution to Leann's last-minute dilemma

Community volunteerism. Help coach little league or soccer. Be part of the beautification project for your community's downtown area, participate in cancer walks, food drives, and other charity events. Not only will you be doing some amazing and worthwhile things, you will be establishing for yourself a reputation that says you care about the needs and wellbeing of others and that you know the importance of giving back to the community. You will also be meeting other business people in the community who can prove to be useful to you for future projects, job changes, and career development goals you have for yourself.

Volunteering to participate in the Relay for Life was something Gwen did to honor the memory of three family members and a close friend who had all died because of cancer. While walking, she met several people who all shared her sense of loss and desire to do what they could to raise money to help find a cure for cancer and for programs for survivors and their families.

One of the people Gwen met was a representative for the Cancer Society in another state. This woman made a point to participate in these events in different towns each year. She did so to hear the stories of other people, which she would then use (with their permission) in brochures, videos, and so on. Gwen, a freelance writer, was intrigued by what she did and said she would love to talk to her in the future if there were any openings in her department. The two talked more about their respective jobs and career goals, and ended the night wishing each other well.

Fast-forward nearly a year. Gwen received and email from the woman she'd met at the relay walk. She was asking Gwen if she would be interested in coming to work with her. Gwen ended up taking the job and is now two years into a job she loves. She also knows that this job is just the beginning of using her talents as a writer to climb the ladder of success in the field of business writing.

Company volunteerism. Play on the company softball team. Organize and/or volunteer to build a float or walk in the town Christmas parade; handing out candy and promotional gifts to parade watchers. Participate in and/or organize a company sponsored event such as school supplies for impoverished families, sponsorship of the high school band or ball team, visiting schools to talk about careers in your company, and things of this nature. Your willingness to represent the company you work for speaks VOLUMES about your views of the people you work for. You see them as more than just a paycheck. You see them as an extension of yourself; something every CEO and HR person looks for when deciding who to promote.

Three people were up for a promotion with a local news station. All three were faithful and diligent employees. Two had over five years of experience, the other individual had barely three. The person with barely three years of experience received the promotion.

After thanking her director for being selected, she asked why she had been chosen over the other more experienced candidates. The man replied by saying that experience wasn't as important to him as dedication to the station. He noted that the newly-promoted young woman was selected because of her obvious enthusiasm to be part of the company 'family'.

LinkedIn. LinkedIn (https://www.linkedin.com) is an excellent way to make yourself accessible to the masses. It is easy to put your profile together and post it on this business networking site. Once you have your profile set up you can search for 'connections' by putting in individual's names, company names, or even interests.

You can join groups based on your profession and interests; giving you an additional outlet for resources specific to your needs.

I've already mentioned it, but I'll say it again—this book wouldn't be happening if not for a LinkedIn connection.

Social Media. Other social networks such as Facebook can be very helpful, but PLEASE, use them wisely. I can think of several instances in which old friends reconnected on Facebook and went on to use that connection as a networking tool for their professional life.

Many people I know who use Facebook have both a personal page and a business page. This is probably the best thing to do in order to keep your personal life separate from your professional one, but even then, you need to be very careful about what you post on your personal page. I cannot tell you how many people I know personally who have been passed over for jobs, gotten put on probation or fired from a job, or who have lost accounts and clients because of pictures that were in poor taste or rude and degrading comments they have posted.

This is NOT to say your personal social media accounts cannot and should not be a place for you to share your thoughts and opinions. You have a right to express your political, religious, and personal thoughts and views. But what you don't have a right to do is bash those of others. So, when using your social media as a platform for anything, remember it is out there for anyone and everyone to see. Even if you are mindful of having solid security measures in place, things still get out.

Trade shows and conventions. Trade shows and conventions can be excellent sources for networking and meeting your career goals. Attendance at these events requires you to actually attend seminars and displays if you expect to make them work for you. You also need to break the ice, introduce yourself, talk a little shop, ask questions, and exchange business cards with as many people as possible.

Doug and Lucy had been talking about relocating back to their hometown. Doug's parents needed care and attention, and the two-hour driving distance was beginning to be a problem.

Lucy worked from home selling her crafty food creations online and to area businesses. She had no qualms about being able to establish and grow her business wherever they lived. Doug, on the other hand, was a real estate agent. He wasn't too sure he would be able to transition into the market and establish a client base. But while at a trade show, he met a commercial real estate agent from his hometown. When they discovered they shared a common bond over the community, the man asked Doug if he would be interested in joining his team. The town was in the early stages of a major development that included three new subdivisions, a new shopping district, and a revitalization of the historic downtown area.

Doug and Lucy talked and decided to make the move. The fact that they encountered the opportunity at a trade show was a sure sign that it was meant to be. To date, it has been everything they could have hoped for and more. The added bonus of being able to care for Doug's parents is something money cannot buy.

Professional Associations. This falls in line with community volunteerism, but on a scale that requires a little more commitment. Belonging to a professional association may require a membership fee and regular attendance to meetings (usually monthly) in order to make your membership genuine.

Consider identifying a professional association that is related to your college major or field of interest.

Are you getting the message that networking is a multi-faceted 'event'? I hope so. I also hope you take proper advantage of each of them to the extent they apply to your specific career and career goals.

Moving on, the next thing you need to know about successful networking is how to network—how to *do* networking so that you get the most out of it.

How to make networking work for YOU

Knowing why to network and where to go to network (the strategies and resources we just talked about) is only as good as the effort you put into using them and knowing how to use them to your advantage.

In order to accomplish the ultimate goals of networking you need to:

Know yourself

Take a few minutes to review the previous chapter that covers this topic and review the answers to the questions and evaluations you took. Additionally, consider the following:

- **Turn your interests into networking assets**. If you don't like children, don't volunteer to coach a little league team. If you aren't the outdoors type, don't volunteer for picking up litter. If cooking is your thing, volunteer to work in the kitchen at a civic event. If you went to college on a soccer scholarship, then volunteer to coach or ref the little league teams and/or play on the adult intramural league.
- **Put your abilities to work for you**. If you are an accountant, volunteering to help seniors with their taxes is a great way to network. If you throw a great party, serve on the committee to host community-wide parties for kids or your office Christmas party. Use these as opportunities to network by asking for door prize donations, sponsorships, and so forth.

- **Know your values.** Work values are something you need to have and know. Are you willing to work weekends on a regular basis? Does excessive overtime not bother you? Are you okay with working in an environment that is less structured? Can you work past the office drama and politics that often take place and aren't really addressed? Will you be offended if your place of employment plays Christian music? Will you consider it against your civil rights if there is a strict dress code? You need to decide these things and take them into consideration when establishing network connections. There's no need to work toward building a relationship if you aren't interested in working with that person.

- **Focus on your strengths.** Potential employers are more interested in what you can do than what you can't do. Need I say more?

- **DO NOT be afraid to let your personal attributes shine.** Do you have a knack for remembering names? Don't be afraid to make that known. Are you a creative thinker who doesn't let the little details get pushed aside? People will want to know that about you. Are you bi-lingual? This is an asset that is becoming more and more popular and in-demand. Were you at the top of your class? Have you traveled abroad and/or have family connections in the international business community? Make sure your contacts know who you are as a person (but not too personal). Knowing these things makes you more 'real' than just a name and facts on a resume.

- **DO NOT neglect making your qualifications known.** Again…potential employers and business associates are just as interested in what you can do for them as you are in knowing what they can do for you. Why? Because networking is a two-way street.

Know your Field of Interest

It does no good to network if you don't know what you are going after—or at least have an idea of what you are looking for. For example…

Isabella had dreamed of being a teacher for years. But her desire to teach was somewhat different than her peers. Isabella wanted to teach home economics. Do you even know what that is? It is a class where students are taught to cook, sew, balance a checkbook, make smart shopping decisions, and other household tasks. Isabella's great-grandma, grandma, and mom all taught home-economics and she wanted to follow suit. She loved everything about it and she wanted very much to keep up this family tradition.

So what was the problem? Many school systems no longer offered home-economics (which was renamed 'consumer sciences' a few years back). Many school systems chose to ditch these classes in favor of more STEM classes; thus limiting Isabella's geographical opportunities.

In all honesty, knowing the teaching industry is now leaning so heavily toward STEM-type classes wouldn't have changed Isabella's mind. But her experience is an excellent example of the importance of knowing your industry in order to be able to 'cash in' on the greatest possible number of job opportunities.

Knowing your industry includes:

- **Being familiar with the <u>Occupational Outlook Handbook and O*NET.</u>** Using industry-information websites. O*NET is an excellent website for doing a bit of industry research https://www.onetonline.org/ and https://www.bls.gov/ooh/.
- **Familiarizing yourself with company websites**. Know what their mission is. Know what their goals are. Know what aspects of the industry they focus on.

- **Knowing a little bit about the people you are building relationships with.** While the bulk of this should come through your interactions with them, it pays to do a bit of homework on the side. You know what I'm talking about: Google them, look them up on social media sites, etc... Knowing a bit about the people you are connecting with can save you some embarrassing and awkward moments. It can also save time and energy. Why bother investing in a relationship if you wouldn't be comfortable working with that person?

- **Knowing your goals.** You need to have a game plan for your career in order to know which direction to take your networking. Now, I realize that sometimes the path we set out on isn't the one we stay on—and that's fine. But you have to have an intended destination (basic plan) in order to get started. For example, someone starting their career in library science needs to have goals in regard to whether they want to work in a public library system or in a more professional and specialized setting such as a law library or library of archived historical documents. Knowing these things about yourself will enable you to head in the proper direction toward making connections that can help you reach your goals.

- **Knowing what questions to ask can make all the difference in a successful connection and one that is not.** Asking someone in the healthcare industry to weigh in on tax cuts or deregulating the pharmaceutical industry might not be very wise. In doing so you open the door to controversial debates and you invite these people to judge your ability based on your feelings (or even perceived feelings).

- **Having realistic expectations.** Entering the job force or a new career path naturally places you on the bottom of the totem pole, so to speak. You shouldn't expect to be hired for anything more than an entry-level job. Hey, we all have to start someplace and expecting anything more gives you the appearance of 'suffering' from the 'disease' of entitlement. Starting at the bottom and working your way up isn't a bad thing. In doing so you learn humility, learn the industry from the 'ground up', appreciate the effort and determination it takes to advance in your field, and you *earn* the reputation you make for yourself.

Additionally, when making sure you are fully prepared to effectively network, you need to remember to:

- **Always keep your eyes and ears open**. You never know who you will meet at any given time. So be ready.

- **Explain the reason for your call/email**. Always have a purpose for every interaction. You will always give a version of your marketing message even if it is more conversational than formal.

- **Have some questions and comments prepared in advance**. This is crucial when you have time to prepare for the encounter/interaction. Even if the encounter is by chance or impromptu, you need to have some general questions and comments prepared at all times.

- **Establish rapport**. Be friendly. Be approachable. Be polite. Be interested and engaging. Use the right body language.

- **Ask for names of other professionals in the field**- A lot of people do not think to do this. But you need to. How else do you expect to expand your network? Get in the habit of asking for additional contacts after every meeting you have. Let them know how much you appreciated their advice or insight and let them know that you are eager to receive more information.

- **Follow up in a timely manner**- Sending a follow-up thank you email within 24-48 hours shows initiative and respect. Get in the habit of sending a thank-you email after every interaction. Ask for business cards to get their contact information. Also ask if you can connect with them on LinkedIn.

- **Prepare your Personal Marketing Message**. This is that 'elevator speech' we talked about earlier.

- **Dress for success**. You don't have to have designer labels but your clothes must absolutely be neat, clean, modest, somewhat fashionable, and well-fitting.

- **Go beyond your industry**. Don't lock yourself in. While some professions, such as marketing and finance, naturally have opportunities in several industries, others such as healthcare and the entertainment industry are seen as fairly closed. Don't do this to yourself. For example, I know a number of healthcare workers that go outside the box by working on cruise ships or as traveling doctors and nurses for mission organizations. I also know drama, art, and music majors who work at resorts either as entertainers or teaching classes.

- **Revisit your personal branding and goals on a yearly basis**. Don't be a slave to your initial goals and plans. As you take each step in your career, reevaluate whether or not you are going in the direction you want to go.

Wow! That's a lot of information, isn't it? I hope you're not in information overload mode. If so, I apologize. But this it is all very important. So take a few deep breaths and then keep going. I promise it's worth it.

Networking Worksheet

Use the charts below to get your networking strategy started and to help you maintain the relationships you build.

Friends/Peers/Family/Neighbors

Name	Relation	Phone/Email	Contact Outcome	Follow-Up/Thank you?

Former or Current Employers/Co-workers

Name	Relation	Phone/Email	Contact Outcome	Follow-Up/Thank you?

Faculty/Coaches/Advisors/Former Teachers

Name	Relation	Phone/Email	Contact Outcome	Follow-Up/Thank you?

Potential Networking Contacts- People You Want to Connect With (Alum)

Name	Relation	Phone/Email	Contact Outcome	Follow-Up/Thank you?

Common Questions to ask:

- What is a typical work day like?

- How and why did you choose this career?

- What are the most and least rewarding aspects of your job?

- What are the most important skills and abilities required for this career or job?

- What do you wish you knew (but didn't) when you first contemplated this career?

- Do you foresee any significant changes in the future?

- What is your educational and professional background?

- What type of education/training is needed for this job?

<table>
<tr><td>Personal Notes</td></tr>
</table>

Chapter 7:

The Job Search

Oh, the agony of the job search! It is something you look forward to and dread…all at the same time. The anticipation of actually adulting combined with the fear of rejection that makes you want to run and hide.

I wish I could tell you that the job search process is fun. I wish I could tell you that the biggest problem you will face during this process is deciding which amazing offer to take. I wish I could tell you how long you will have to look before finding the job you want. I also wish I could tell you that the first job you take (or the next job you take if you are in the process of changing jobs) will be your perfect job. Unfortunately, I cannot tell you any of these things, because I'd be lying and we both know lying always ends up getting you into trouble.

So instead, I'll be honest. The process of finding a job can be long, tiresome, frustrating, and very overwhelming and stressful. Submitting a resume and being granted an interview sends your hopes soaring. Not hearing back…or hearing you didn't get the job causes your confidence level to plummet. Then you submit another resume and get another interview. Hope is once again on the rise. You get a call back. Hope and expectations go even higher. You don't get the job. You're devastated. After taking a little time to collect yourself, you do it all again. But this time you get the job!!! It's time to do the happy dance; followed (almost) immediately by the nervous jitters. Will you be able to do the job? Will your boss and coworkers like you? Will the job be everything you want and need it to be? And what should you do if it isn't?

So remember: As you go through the process of finding a job, keep in mind that it is just that—a process. And like any other process the job search process takes time, persistence, consistency, and sometimes it even requires thinking outside the box. It is also enough to push your stress level through the roof and make you a little crazy. The good news in all of this is that it doesn't have to be that way—or rather there are steps you can take to lessen the negative effects searching for a job can have on your body and mind. The most important one being **self-care.**

Self-care is a term that simply means you take care of your body and your mind. How? By **eating a healthy diet, getting plenty of exercise, getting the right amount of sleep, taking time to relax and enjoy family, friends, and hobbies, and taking time to just relax.**

We understand the importance of doing these things (even if we don't do them) when we are working. But often times when we are involved in the process of finding a job we don't take the time to do these things. I'm not completely sure why we don't. Maybe we don't think we have the time. Maybe we don't think we have the 'luxury' of slacking off until we are gainfully employed. Maybe we have such a severe case of tunnel vision that we don't see anything but applications, resumes, and interviews.

The truth of the matter, though, is that we need to see the process of searching for a job like that of a full-time job; one with set hours, lunch breaks, and nights and weekends free to do whatever you feel like doing (except searching for a job). If you don't, you are doing your body and mind a great disservice and could actually be jeopardizing your chances of getting the job you want. Think about it—if you are exhausted and stressed-out, how well do you think you are going to do in an interview? How great an impression are you going to make if you are bleary-eyed, yawning, and your skin is pale from lack of blood flow and healthy foods? I rest my case.

Self-care essentials

I want you to take a look at what the Mayo Clinic lists as the signs of stress on one's body and mind. As you look through the list consider how many of these things currently describe you. Be honest. If you are experiencing two or more (total), you need to make some changes…and quick.

I said it once, I'll say it again…you aren't doing yourself or your prospective employers any favors by neglecting your self-care. In fact, you are only making things worse.

<u>Body:</u>

- Headache
- Muscle tension
- Chest pain
- Fatigue
- Upset stomach
- Sleep Problems

<u>Behavior:</u>

- Diet changes
- Angry outbursts
- Drug or alcohol abuse
- Tobacco use
- Social isolation
- Anxiety

<u>Mood:</u>

- Restless-ness
- Lack of moti-vation or focus
- Irritability or anger
- Sadness or dep-ression

If you are experiencing any of these symptoms (or even if you aren't), I strongly suggest getting a physical. Tell the doctor how you are feeling and why so he/she can help you come up with a plan to alleviate your symptoms and get you on the right track for better physical, emotional, and mental health. This way you will be ready to give 100% of your skills and talents to your new job (the one you *will* get).

FYI: If you are still in college or just graduated, you will likely still be covered under your parent's insurance. Since most insurance providers include a free yearly physical in their coverage, the exam will not cost you anything. If you aren't covered by insurance, there are free clinics on campus or in most communities. In other words, don't let a lack of funds be your excuse for not getting a physical.

Why we get stressed

Once you admit you are allowing stress and anxiety to get to you, the next essential step is to pinpoint *why* you are feeling so stressed.

"What? Are you serious?" you ask. "What do you mean I need to figure out why I'm stressed? I'm stressed because I don't have a job!"

I know you're stressed because you don't have a job…yet. But there's a reason or reasons you are stressed out about not having a job. And *that's* what we're going to look at next.

Internal & external pressure. Pressure you are putting on yourself can be either rational or irrational. Remember the Social Media syndrome? Feeling like everyone else's life is perfect. Feeling like everyone is getting on with their life…everyone but you. You have student loans to pay off and they want their money whether you have a job or not. You've worked hard for your degree and you want to use it. You are ready to be independent and make your own way in life. You want to settle down and get married, but doing so without a job is irresponsible. Only lazy or unqualified people are unemployed.

And then there are the pressures from other people. **Parents**—I didn't spend all that money on your education for nothing…did I? **Grandparents**—make me proud, okay? **Peers**—Really? No offers yet? Hhhmmmm…. **Partner or spouse**—we can't set a date until we know we have jobs OR the bills are going to keep coming whether you are working or not. **Everyone means well**—don't get discouraged. Something will come along. Rome wasn't built in a day. Maybe you've got your expectations set too high. They don't know what they're missing out on by not hiring you. Maybe you need to tweak your resume.

When trying to rationalize and justify the pressures weighing you down, please remember that you are where you are supposed to be right now. Where you are now is just a step toward where you are headed next.

Fear of the Unknown. What if I get rejected? We all have at some point. Remember, though, that a rejection simply means the job wasn't right for you and you weren't right for the job. It just isn't meant to be. Rejection does NOT mean you are a reject. Rejection doesn't mean you are a failure. Rejection doesn't mean you are unworthy of employment. Rejection doesn't mean your education was a waste of time and money. And most importantly…**without rejection you would never truly appreciate what it means to be accepted.**

Competition. Who else is applying for the position? How many are applying? Hundreds? Thousands. It really doesn't matter, does it? No, it doesn't. What matters is that you do your best and present your best self. Don't compare yourself to anyone but yourself.

Interview performance. How did I do on the interview? When will I hear back from them? Will I hear back from them at all? Did I look okay? Did I sound like I knew what I was talking about? Did I answer their questions correctly? Did I give off the right vibes? Did I have food in my teeth? Did I appear confident or did I seem cocky? Was I too quiet? Did they think I was weak or unmotivated?

New workplace woes. Will I like my new work environment? Will it be friendly or competitive? Will there be a lot of drama? Will my co-workers like me? Will I like them? Will my boss be pleasant to work for? Will he/she like me? Will they be a micromanager? Will I be able to meet and exceed their expectations?

Financial pressures. I can only live with my parents for so long. I really don't want to move back home. I have loans to pay back. I need a new car. My parents can no longer carry me on their insurance.

Getting the job. I got it! Can I really do it? How do I transition from carrying a backpack to a briefcase? How do I go from being a student to an employee? How do I know how much to contribute to my retirement account? I'm officially an adult! Yikes!

Having to eliminate options. Having to choose which job to take is a good problem to have, but how do I know I'm making the right decision? What if I make the wrong one? What if the job I take turns out to be a disaster? What if….

Separation from social groups. Now that we've graduated all of my friends have moved away. My friends don't have time for me anymore. We don't have much in common anymore—not like we did in college. Should I consider my coworkers my friends? Should we hang out after work?

Fear of failure. What if I never find a job? What if I can't find a job in my field? What if I get fired from my job? What if I really mess up? What if I end up hating my job? What if I end up hating the profession I got a degree in?

Every single one of these reasons for getting stressed out is both justified and unjustified. The difference is decided by:

- How you handle your thoughts and feelings
- Your unique situation

- How you deal with each of these issues

For example, there is absolutely nothing wrong with feeling a certain weight of responsibility toward not living with your parents and being able to begin paying back your student loans. Using these feelings as motivation to not give up searching for a job or to possibly reevaluate your job search techniques is a good thing. Letting your feelings drive you to the point of being physically ill and having panic attacks…not so much.

Another example of using these factors in a positive way is separation from social groups. Sometimes recent college grads whose job search is taking a little longer than they think it should try to hang on to their 'youth' by continuing to socialize like many college students socialize. You know what I'm talking about…partying until the wee hours and sleeping most of the day, or gaming for hours on end. When you say no to this type of socializing; taking the more mature route of sobriety and a good night's sleep, you are using the reasons we just categorized maturely and responsibly. Go you!

In the movie, "Miss Congeniality 2", Sandra Bullock is struggling with her new-found fame as a role model for girls and young women and a spokesperson for the FBI. Her struggles are mainly due to the fact that she can't seem to find the right balance between being the tough, often too-manly, go-with-your-gut-instinct agent she is naturally, with being the poised, well-spoken, feminine agent the FBI wants to present to the public.

In one particular scene, Bullock, whose character's name is Gracie Hart, tells a middle-school student who is trying to learn it's okay to be herself, too, that "…people only care about people who care about themselves." While Gracie's overall philosophy was a bit skewed, her worlds ring true. People, aka potential employers, will definitely care about (take more notice) applicants who obviously care about themselves *by taking care of themselves.*

Self-care, or the lack of it, shows. What do you want prospective employers to see when they look at you?

Coping with the stresses of the job search

We've just acknowledged the fact that there are stress factors related to looking for and finding a job that aren't going anywhere. We've also looked at what those stress factors are and why they have the ability to affect you the ways in which they do. Now let's take a few minutes to look at how to cope with the stresses of searching for a job. After all, what kind of self-help book would this be if it didn't offer solutions to your problems?

Start Early. The early birds really do catch the best worms. Ideally, you want to begin your search months before you will actually enter the work force. Some college students start as early as the summer after their sophomore year by working as summer interns. These internships allow students to realistically evaluate their chosen career path AND give them a head start in establishing a presence and getting their 'name out there' with potential employers.

Jordan is a great example of what this looks like. Following his sophomore year in college, he applied for and was accepted into an internship program for computer engineering majors at a MAJOR corporation. He loved it! The work…the work environment…the location…everything. And they loved Jordan. In fact, before he left that first week of August, they offered him a spot for the following summer. The following summer went just as well. And when he got ready to leave then, they offered him a full-time job to start three weeks after graduation. Four years later he is still there and is now training and working with the intern program that got his foot in the door.

If internships aren't an option for you or if an internship results in letting you know where you *don't* want to work, think about this: if you want a June start date, depending on when the employer is looking to fill the position, you need to start your search at least 3-6 months prior to that. Even if you are not actually applying for a position, you still need to begin networking and researching your field of interest.

Understand that it's a process. Processes take time, so you need to be patient. You need to give employers time to review applicants and research those they put on the short-list. You also need to respect the fact that while they are looking for employees they still have other duties to do as well. You also need to remember that the process is going to involve rejection. That's just part of it. On your end, the process involves persistence, consistency, patience, confidence, and ingenuity.

Set realistic expectations/goals. This is crucial for keeping the level of disappointment and discouragement as low as possible. Setting unrealistic goals is just setting yourself up for both. So please make sure you aren't trying to reach for an unknown galaxy when you should be reaching for the stars. For example, if you are looking to start a job on June 1 and you just started looking at the end of May, chances are very slim that you will meet your June 1 deadline. Or if you apply for a job that is clearly an upper-level job for those with several years of experience and you have little or none, you really don't have a right to be disappointed when you don't get the position—or even an interview.

When setting your goals and expectations, know your worth and be confident with your experience, but understand and be aware of the requirements for the positions you apply for. I've also found that it is always better to be able to meet and exceed the requirements and expectations for a position than to fall short of them. Employees who meet and exceed their boss's expectations are the employees who get promoted. The ones that fall short go nowhere, except out the door.

Have a plan. It is important to create a strategy that works for you. The key to this plan being successful is making sure it is feasible, reasonable, and consistent. You may decide, like some people I know, to treat the job search like a full-time job. You begin your day at 8am and end your day at 5 pm. During that time period you apply for positions, send some emails, schedule interviews, make follow-up calls if applicable, and actually go on interviews. You also take a lunch break and afternoon break each day and don't take your 'work' home with you when the day is over.

Sometimes this strategy is unrealistic for your chosen field. Some fields are so specialized that it doesn't lend itself to this method. Other jobs have specific hiring periods; meaning you have to hit it hard during that time frame and wait. Or maybe you are working part-time (or even full-time) at a job you took to carry you over until you get the job you want. If this is your situation, you will understandably have to tailor your job search plan to fit your schedule. The important thing is that you have a plan and stick to it.

Utilize various methods. In almost every situation there is more than one way to get the job done…and done right. Searching for job is one of those things. Failing to take advantage of the various methods for finding a job can severely limit your options and greatly increase the time it takes to find and be hired for the job that is right for you. What are these options?

- **Networking.** Failure to network can really hinder your search. By making connections through networking, you can accumulate names to go with your applications. Using these people as references, however, should only be done with their permission. Dropping their name in a cover letter, in answering a question on an application, or during an interview, without their permission, is completely unacceptable.

For example: "I met ___________ _________ when we both volunteered as cheerleaders for the Special Olympics. She really impressed me and shared some thoughts with me that made me even more confident that I am well-suited for _____________.

I know we spent a great deal of time on networking, so I will end this by saying: **It's what you know + Who you know + Who knows you** ☺

- **Online job searches.** There are a number of websites that have proven to be the answer to a lot of people's prayers for a job. I've been singing the praises of LinkedIn, and I will remind you once more to not ignore the possibilities it holds for you. But there are others that provide more direct leads to jobs that are open NOW. These are just a few of the more popular job websites you can use in addition to state employment websites, federal employment websites, and those geared specifically to your chosen field. Some of these include:
    - https://www.linkedin.com
    - https://www.glassdoor.com/index.htm
    - https://www.indeed.com/
- **Tap into your support system.** Don't be afraid to ask family members for job leads, friends, parents of friends, people in your neighborhood, people you go to church with, people who work out at the same gym, and those you know from other social outlets.
- **Know where to look.** Don't overlook the obvious when looking for a job: job fairs, field-specific websites, going directly to the company websites of places you might like to work, trade shows, college job posting boards, and good old-fashioned word of mouth.

Make sure your job search documents are in order. Your **resume** needs to be clean, current, complete, yet concise, and completely truthful. I am not going to go into detail on how to create an effective resume. There are plenty of resources to help you do that. But I will list for you the basics of an effective and professional-looking resume. Your resume is of great importance because it is usually the first impression you will make on a prospective employer, so make sure it's a good one.

- 1-2-page document is typically preferred
- Section headings should be consistent
- Font size and style should be consistent
- Make sure it is a TAILORED Resume. (More on this topic later)
- Do not include your references or "References available upon request". Submit your references on a separate document or list them on the application (if applicable).
- Have it critiqued for proper grammar and spelling

Additionally, you need to:

- **Know your audience**. Who are you writing your resume for? (tailoring is mentioned before) Know what your industry is looking for.
- **Know yourself**. A resume is not about listing what you did. It is about showing your impact to a company. For instance, instead of only mentioning tasks, think about the skills you demonstrated and results you achieved (accomplishments)
- **Be truthful**. Honesty and integrity are 2 very important components for an effective resume.
- **Identify professionals** (networking contacts) who could review your document and possibly share it with others. This step represents the importance of networking. Applying online should NOT be your only job search strategy. You want to make sure your resume gets into the hands of someone who will notice it.

- **Share your Professional and Academic Story.** Your demographic information and the city you grew up in are not important to an employer. They want to know what your skills and accomplishments are, not hobbies and interests.
- **Make sure your References are current and applicable**. References are more common than letters of recommendations for the job search. It is professionally appropriate to ask your references for their permission to be listed on your application. *Trick: At the beginning of your job search, contact your references and ask them if they will be a reference for you. If they say yes, let them know that you are beginning your job search process and will be listing them on several applications. Let them know that they may be receiving notifications from several employers. By doing this, you do not have to remember to contact them after every position you apply to.

Including a Cover letter

Do you need to include a cover letter? Do employers really read cover letters? It is really hard to say. My advice would be that if it is requested, submit one. If it is not requested but you want to submit one anyway, great! Regardless of the reason, if you submit a cover letter remember the brand characteristic, "consistency." You want to make sure your cover letter is strengthening your qualifications vs. hindering them. Take your time in writing one. Do not rush! Make sure that it is tailored and showcasing your relevant experiences:

- 1st paragraph: Tell why you are writing, state the position title, tell why you are interested in the company
- 2nd paragraph: State your degree, graduation date. Reference your skills and experiences to the job description. Show how you are qualified.
- 3rd paragraph: refer readers to your resume. Ask for what you want. Thank them for their consideration

Now about tailoring your resume…

Having a tailored job search will make your job search process a lot easier. Here are a few reasons of why this is so and how to make sure yours is tailored to near-perfection.

Gone are the days (if they ever existed) where you list every accomplishment and experience you've had on your resume. Employers do not want a book and they don't care about the duties of your job as a caddy when you were a teenager. Employers typically take about 20-30 seconds to make an initial scan of a resume. They know what they are looking for in a potential candidate before they even review a document, so they are looking to see if any key words or phrases are there to grab their attention. If so, the resume will get a closer look later. If not, you are pretty much guaranteed it will be tossed. Therefore, you need to make their job as easy as possible and make your resume one that will get that second look…and beyond. How do you do that? By following these steps:

1. Print out the job description or posting. Use the job posting as a cheat sheet.

2. Scan the job posting twice. During the first scan, you are trying to determine if the job is worth pursuing. Your second scan will be longer. Begin to highlight all the skills, experiences, and qualifications that the employer is looking for. The skills will probably range from technical (hard) to transferrable (soft).

3. Identify the skills, experiences, and qualifications you have that are applicable to the job and list them. You also want to review your education, work experience, volunteer, internships, skills, projects, and honors and awards you have received that should make you a top contender for the position.

4. Look at your resume. Is it a true and accurate representation of you?

5. Does it directly address the position you are applying for without sounding like you've copied and pasted the job description? Which, by the way, you should not do. This means that you will probably have multiple versions of your resume. That's okay. Tailoring can be time-consuming, but it is well worth it.

Now let's take another minute to discuss the cover letter. A cover letter is NOT intended to be a summary of your resume. The cover letter should be more about the job posting itself and your interest in working for the company. Here is an example of a great opening paragraph for a cover letter:

To: Chris Forrester:

The name LOWE has been a popular one in my family for years when it comes to boats. Whether I've been fishing, skiing, or just relaxing on the water, I've done it on a Lowe boat. So when I learned of the opening in your marketing division, I immediately decided to send my resume and request that I be considered for the position.

Do you see how the opening statement not only expressed a personal interest in the company, but also 'insinuated' that the applicant was skilled in the field of advertising and marketing?

On the other hand, some cover letters would need to take a more formal approach…

To: Dr. Benjamin Widener:

Hello, my name is ____________. Over the course of the last several months I have been troubled by the fact that many of our school systems are severely lacking in funding; making it difficult to give students the resources for learning they deserve. My introduction to this problem came from a report I read about loan forgiveness programs for teachers and one on school district dissolution because of a lack of funding. It is because I truly believe these students deserve every opportunity afforded to those in more financially-secure districts that I am applying for a position with

____________________________.

This opening paragraph is more formal, yet captures the attention of the reader because it displays a passion for the profession while honestly stating that they understand the benefits that go with it, i.e. loan forgiveness.

It is also imperative that you review the job posting. You want to be sure you understand what the primary focus of the job description is. Once you know that, you need to choose to *focus* on two of your skills and/or experiences and simply list the other pertinent skills and experiences. For example, if you are applying for a marketing position, one of the experiences you should focus on is the marketing internship you did. In addition to your marketing internship you would want to focus on the digital marketing experience you gained working in the university's recruiting office as a web designer.

Next on your agenda should be to provide new information that will really make you stand out to the employer. Think about the skills that you gained from your internship. Identify those and briefly relate how they are relevant to the job you are applying for.

One last thing…cover letters can take a while to write. Hint… If you are applying to the same position at different companies, the only paragraph that you will need to tailor is the first one.

When tailoring your resume you need to make sure you have a **Marketing Message.** This is the same message you use when you introduce yourself in a networking situation. To review the concept of a marketing message, please review branding chapter for information on what it is and how to create one. Remember, though, for the purposes of tailoring, you want to make sure you are communicating skills, experiences, and accomplishments that are relevant to *that position.*

Why Tailor

At this point if you are rolling your eyes and heaving sighs of that's-too-much-work-for-me, you need to keep in mind what I said a few paragraphs ago: employers devote no more than a half a minute (30 seconds) to a resume before deciding which ones deserve a closer look. So why in the world wouldn't you do everything possible to make sure yours gets that second look?

Other reasons you need to tailor your resume include what I'll call an **Applicant Tracking System.** If you choose to apply to an online posting, be prepared to encounter an Applicant Tracking system. A lot of companies are using them. Think of it as a large scanner that application documents go through. Remember, employers have identified what they are looking for in an applicant and have included this information in the job posting. After your resume is reviewed by the tracking system to determine if your resume meets the basic requirements, it then passes it through to the next step in the process. By making sure you have tailored your resume accordingly, you greatly increase your chances of making it past the tracking system and into the actual hands of those responsible for sifting through the resumes to find the best fit for the position. And that may be you! If your resume isn't tailored, your resume will most likely be tossed before anyone actually ever lays eyes on it.

Tailoring your resume also lets companies know you are taking the process seriously and personally. You aren't just mass-mailing resumes to anyone and everyone that might possibly hire you. You are seriously searching for a job that fits you. Employers like that.

Tailoring your resume is like buying clothes that fit. You do so in order to present yourself in the very best 'light'.

When networking and the application process cross paths…or do they

One question people often ask themselves is when or if networking should be part of the *application* process when searching for a job. In other words, how far do you take the networking conversations in the direction of "I'd like to have a job with your company."

The answer to that question is that it depends. Each situation is somewhat unique and needs to be evaluated for its appropriateness. Applying online and then following up with a networking contact is often a great way to make sure your resume makes it through the first round and there is nothing wrong with that. But be mindful of who you are contacting. Networking contacts that are 'just' employees may not have anything to offer in the job-filling department. So when deciding whether or not to make a follow up call or send an email, you need to know if it will make a difference.

Speaking of a follow-up call…

Making a follow-up call or email on the status of your application is always appropriate. In the event, you haven't heard back from the company (one way or the other) you should follow-up seven to ten days after the deadline for applications has passed. If there is not a posting or application deadline given, two weeks is a pretty standard waiting period before following up with either a call or email.

Filling out an application

Most applications are filled out online these days. Very few places are going to ask you to put pen to paper. This is definitely to your advantage, as it reduces the possibility of your application being discarded for being illegible or full of spelling errors. But filling out online applications do require more from you than just hitting the send button. When filling out an application, always remember to:

- Keep a copy of the application in a file on your computer.
- Keep a spreadsheet that will allow you to keep track of the applications you send, when you send them, follow-up notes, interview notes, etc.…
- Never leave anything blank. Even if the answer is N/A, don't leave it blank—unless it instructs you to do so.
- Make sure your email settings are such that replies aren't routed to your spam box
- Before you start sending out applications and resumes, clean up anything suspect, embarrassing, or inappropriate from your social media.
- Make sure your phone's voice mail greeting is professional sounding.
- Remember you are where you are supposed to be now because it is preparing you to take the next step in your career journey.

Take a few minutes to answer the following questions in order to help you get (and stay) in the right mindset for the process of searching for a job.

How are you feeling about your job search? (Be specific)

Identify some self-care strategies you can utilize when you get stressed

What is your job search plan/strategy?

Why are you interested in your field of interest?

What are your strongest skills?

What experiences can you share that demonstrate your skills?

What type of work environment are you looking for?

Which occupations are you going to research?

What are the current events affecting your areas of interest?

What are the relevant professional and trade associations?

Locate useful websites on the internet

Identify key employers

IMPORTANT: Use these key thoughts and questions to help organize your job search process. In doing so you will save time and energy—both yours and that of prospective employers.

Chapter 8:

Effective Interviewing: Bringing Your Best Game to the Interview

You have filled out application after application and have clicked 'send' to submit more resumes than you care to count. And you've waited for a call or an email saying, "We'd like to schedule a time for an interview…."

For some those words come quickly. For others, not nearly as soon as you'd like. No matter when they come, however, you need to be ready to bring your best game to each and every interview you are granted.

What do you think about when you hear the term 'effective interviewing'? Do you handle yourself in such a way that the interviewer will walk away from the interview with the answers to his/her questions? And will the answers he/she gets make you a favorable contender for the position?

Hopefully you think about what you need to say and do to present yourself as someone equal to the task of filling the position you are applying for.

Effective interviewing is *also* about asking the right questions. While the primary purpose of the interview is to determine from their perspective, whether you are a good fit for the position and for the company overall, you need to be making these same assessments from *your* perspective, as well.

Just like prospective employers comb through the resumes they receive before granting interviews, you need to do your own company research to know whether or not a company will be well-suited to your career goals (long and short-term). You also need to decide whether their mission and overall attitude is conducive to yours, and whether you believe you will feel motivated and useful/valued in the work environment. Some of this can and should be done prior to submitting an application and/or resume. Weed out those that don't meet the criteria you place at the top of your priority list. Once this has been done you will need to do additional research on companies you feel you would like to work for.

Using social media, company websites, and industry-related websites can serve you well in preparing you for an interview. In studying these resources, you can know ahead of time some of the facts and figures regarding the company's methods of operation and management.

Knowing these things will not only make you appear personally interested in the company, but they can serve as a guide in putting together a list of questions to ask (and which not to ask) in regard to the company's future, what they expect from their employees, and so forth.

Preparing for an interview

Preparing for an interview is as important as the interview itself. If it helps, think of each interview as a final for the most difficult or detrimental course you took in college. If you do that, you can then view prepping for the interview as study time prior to the final.

Or if you've been out of school for a couple of years or more and you are interviewing to change jobs or even career paths, think of interview-prepping in the same way you viewed preparing for a presentation at work or presenting a campaign or design to your top client.

Did you get that? Prepping for an interview is IMPORTANT!

The following is a list of general things you need to know and do prior to an interview.

- **Prepare a list of questions you will likely be asked to answer.**
- **Practice answering these questions.**
- **Prepare questions for the employer.**
- **Prepare follow-up questions based on possible answers you will receive.**
- **Decide what materials to have with you (In-person interview).**
  - Extra copies of your resume
  - Your list of questions—you don't want to forget or assume anything
  - Additional references in case the interviewer asks for them
  - A padfolio
  - Breath mints
- **Consider your visual affect**. Make sure you are dressed professionally. Even if the job you are interviewing for lends itself to a more casual dress code, dress professionally—no jeans, t-shirts, shorts, sundresses, low-cut dresses or tops, nothing see-through, hemline no more than 2 inches above the knee, neutral nail polish with no chips, non-descript jewelry, natural-looking makeup, neatly-combed hair, fresh breath, clothes neatly pressed, no over-sized purses and pants secured around your waist
- **Know the time of the interview**. Know ahead of time where to park, which door to enter, which elevator to take to get to the location of the interview, and who to ask for. It is also a good idea to arrive 10 to 15 minutes early; giving you time to find a parking place, use the restroom, and to ask for directions if necessary.

- **Research the company and position.** We've already covered this, but it was worth mentioning again.
- **Practice your handshake**. This may sound silly, but it really is important. Your handshake tells a lot about you.
- **Know who you are interviewing with.** Example: Interviewing with HR vs. Director of the department. Who you are interviewing with sometimes determines which questions you direct to each of them.
- **Remember that your interview starts the moment you step on the property** ☺

Sometimes interviews don't take place face-to-face. Sometimes interviews are done via webcams, using SKYPE, or over the telephone. Interviews of this nature still require the same degree of preparation. Make sure you prepare for the different types of interviews.

Most Common Interview Types

Phone Interviews

- Use notes for asking questions and writing down answers and comments.
- Practice with someone.
- Dress professionally. No, they can't see you, but when you look professional you will act and speak in a more professional manner.
- Make sure your phone is charged. This is no time for a dropped call.
- Silence. Don't worry about a 2-3 second lapse in conversation, but avoid anything longer unless asked to wait while the interviewer looks over something
- No eating allowed, but water is okay.
- Choose a quiet location where you will not be interrupted and noise will not be an issue.

Video Interviews

- A newer type of interview that is typically used in the screening process. This type of interview allows employers to screen multiple candidates while saving time.
- Employers will create a set of interview questions and email you a link to complete the interview.
- You will have a designated amount of time to access and complete the interview.
- Speak slowly, smile, and be confident!

Web Interviews

- Shut down all browsers and open web pages.
- Practice with someone.
- Use notes for asking questions and writing down answers and comments.
- Dress professionally.
- Make sure your equipment works and you have a solid internet connection.
- No food, but water is okay.
- Choose a quiet location where you will not be interrupted and noise will not be an issue.
- Make sure you have a neutral background. You will be on camera ☺

In-Person Interviews

- Bring extra copies of your resume and references.
- Have a pen and padfolio.
- Bring cash for parking.
- Dress professionally.
- Know the location of the interview- Directions are key.
- Bring any other items requested by the employer.
- Ask for a business card at the end of the interview.
- Always send a follow-up thank-you email.

*1-1 interviews are the most frequent types of interviews but be prepared for a panel interview (multiple interviewers) and a second or possibly third round of interviews. Send separate thank you emails to each interviewer.

<u>Meal Interviews</u>- Employers want to know how you interact in a social setting.

- Turn off your cellphone.
- Remember your table manners.
- Follow the lead of the others in your party.
- Order mid-price range and avoid alcohol – always.
- Be polite to the servers and don't order something complicated.
- Don't order something messy.
- Wait to eat until every member of your party is served.
- Know you likely won't get much to eat – you're the star of the party here!

That all-important first impression

You have probably heard it countless times, but you are going to 'hear' it again right now…

You only get one chance to make a first impression, so make sure it's a good one.

The first impression you make on the person interviewing you happens in a matter of mere seconds. In fact, it happens almost as quickly as that first scan of your resume that determines whether they look at it more thoroughly. That's why your first impression should tell them:

- **You are pleasant and confident**. Your smile, direct eye-contact, and mannerly greeting tell them everything they want to know. You are being interviewed for a job—that's reason enough to smile, right? Eye-contact tells them you are confident, trustworthy, willing to learn/listen, capable of doing the job, and that you respect the person speaking to you. Your greeting should be clearly enunciated and a full sentence. EXAMPLE: "Hello, it is a pleasure to meet you." "Hello, I am pleased to meet you and looking forward to our conversation."
- **Speak clearly and correctly**. Do not use the following 'words': "um", "like" "uh", "ya", "uh-hu", "yep", "nope", curse words, expletives, or slang.
- **If possible, initiate the handshake**. A handshake is always in good taste and appropriate. Just be sure it is firm, but not a bone-crusher. And while you don't EVER want to visibly wipe the sweat from your palm before shaking hands, do make sure you are 'dry' prior to extending your hand.
- **Make sure you have been equally pleasant to the receptionist and everyone else you encounter prior to meeting with the interviewer**. You don't want to make a bad impression on possible co-workers. Besides, you don't know that the young woman on the elevator isn't the boss's daughter or your soon-to-be direct supervisor.

Body language

'Speaking' the right body language is as important in the interview process as what you say. Take a look at the following. Make sure you take note of the positive and negative signals when practicing your interview questions.

Body Language 101

Positive Signals	Negative Signals
Eye contact	Tapping fingers
Leaning forward	Crossed arms
Smiling	Fidgeting in chair
Nodding	Looking away
Unclenched fist	Leaning back

So...tell me what you know

You've seen the phrase 'practice answering questions' more than a time or two in this chapter so far. And most likely you agree that doing so is a good idea. But many of you may be wondering what kind of questions you will be asked. What questions should you be practicing giving answers to? That is a perfectly reasonable question to ask, so here is the answer.

During the interview process, you will likely be asked several questions that fall under the category of general and professional questions. Below is a list of some of the common interview questions:

General interview questions

Tell me about yourself. NOTE: Remember your marketing message! This is your opportunity to sell yourself. Highlight your education, work experience, skills, accomplishments and anything that is going to show the employer that you are a fit to their organization.

Why are you interested in our company/position? RESEARCH, RESEARCH, RESEARCH.

What is your greatest strength? Hint: Strengths are essentially skills. Think about those areas where you excel. Is it your communication? Leadership? Organization? Attention to detail? With every strength (or skill) you name, make sure you provide an example of how you have demonstrated that strength. Your examples are what is going to differentiate you from your competition. I recommend preparing at least three strengths in case the interviewer asks for more than one.

What is your greatest weakness? Hint. Mentally Reframe: "What is your greatest area of improvement." This is a tricky interview question for a couple of reasons. 1) Employers are not expecting you to throw yourself under the bus. Instead, they want you to identify an area that you are working to improve. ALWAYS describe how you are taking steps to improve your area of improvement. 2) Employers are not expecting you to list another strength. Again, identify an area that you are working to improve and communicate how you are improving it. Avoid saying lack of confidence, shy, and perfectionist. Focus on a skill area. Like strengths, I recommend preparing at least three weaknesses in case the interviewer asks for more than one.

What are your long and short-term career goals? This response can be relatively broad. Stick to professional growth and development within the company. If your profession requires certain certifications or licenses, you may want to mention obtaining those as well.

Why should we hire you? This is your last opportunity to market your BRAND. You want to convince the employer that you are a fit to their organization.

In addition to these types of questions, the interviewer will ask questions meant to show him/her who you are as a person. What type of personality do you have? How will you handle stress, competition, deadlines, constructive criticism, and similar circumstances and situations? You need to be ready to answer these questions clearly and honestly.

Behavioral interview questions

What do you feel has been your greatest challenge so far—work or life-related?
How did you handle the situation?
If you were placed in the situation of
_______________________, how would you respond?

In learning about your past behavior, a potential employer can learn a great deal about your future behavior. This is important to them because your behavior affects the work environment as well as the quality of your work.

Behavioral Questions
Past Behavior = Best Predictor of Future Behavior ☺

Can you give me an example of a time when your attention to detail was critical?

Tell me about a time you had to use your communication skills to the fullest

Describe the most creative work related project you have completed.

Tell me about a situation where you went above and beyond the expectations set for you.

Tell me about a time in which you had a conflict with a co-worker or group project member.

Describe a situation in which others within your organization depended on you.

Can you tell me about a time you failed at something? What did you learn from that experience?

Can you tell me about a time you disagreed with a manager?

Behavioral interview questions lend themselves to 'story telling'. These 'stories' need to be short, truthful, and to the point. They should never include name-calling, accusations, hearsay, or opinion you cannot pair with facts.

Something I have found useful in telling these types of 'stories' is the STAR Technique. Take a look on the following pages at how it works and practice putting it to use for your job interviews (and other situations, as well).

STAR Technique

S Situation	Describe the background. Provide a context. When? Where?
T Task	Describe the challenge and expectations. What needed to be done? Why?
A Action	Elaborate YOUR specific Action. What did you do? What were your individual contributions?
R Result	Explain the results: accomplishments, recognition, savings, etc. Quantify when possible.

STAR Example

Tell me about a time you had to use your ability to innovate?

S Situation	I was a part of the Customer Service team at my last job. We experienced poor customer satisfaction and several customer complaints due to the inconsistency of the level of service.
T Task	Being one of the most senior team members, I was asked to propose ideas on how to improve the situation.
A Action	First, I reviewed the results of the customer surveys and collected data about what the dissatisfaction was about. I then called a meeting with my peers and I asked their input. Finally, I came up with a list of five ideas to implement changes supporting service improvement and a plan to measure the future performance of the Customer Service department.

R Result	The number of complaints decreased by 20% in the month following the implementation and by 50% 3 months later.

Creating a STAR Story:

Use the space below to write a STAR story based upon one of the behavioral questions you are likely to be asked.

Situation:

Task:

Action:

Results:

Additional things you want to consider when thinking about how your STAR stories will have the greatest positive impact on an interviewer include:

- Don't get stuck in background information. You will need to set the stage, so to speak, but keep it to a minimum.
- Be specific about YOUR role in the situation—not that of others. Don't make yourself out to be the solo superhero of problem solving. It's okay to mention the role others played in the situation. You just don't need to detail their role. YOUR role is what the interviewer is interested in.
- Be sure to end the story with the outcome of the situation and the benefits of that outcome. The outcome of the situation gives the interviewer insight as to what to expect from you in similar situations.
- Keep it SHORT (no more than 2 minutes…TOPS!)
- Prior to the interview, consider the behavioral questions you are likely to be asked and practice your STAR answers. It is only natural to be a bit nervous during an interview. Practicing won't make your level of nervousness nonexistent, but it *will* greatly reduce your discomfort.

Questions you should ask

Once you have answered the questions your interviewer has for you, you will have a chance to ask your interviewer any questions you have for them.

Chances are that some of your questions will be answered during the first part of the interview process. If so, don't ask the question again just because it is on your list. It is also perfectly acceptable to take notes so that you do not have to rely solely on your memory once the interview is over and you are 'processing' the event.

I also want to advise you against asking questions that can be answered by studying their website. Your interviewer expects you to do your homework, so asking questions that you should already have answers to makes you appear inefficient and disinterested. When your turn comes to ask questions, make sure to ask the following if you haven't already been given the answer to them:

- What is a typical day like in the office (or in the field)?
- Is there a transition or training process? How long would that process be?
- How would you describe the office atmosphere?
- Why did you want to join this organization?
- What do you feel is the most unique attribute of this organization?
- What do you appreciate most about working here?
- What do you consider to be the most important qualities for the person who fills this position?
- What are the overall long-term goals for the organization?

Preparation is to an interview what location is to real estate…nearly everything. But let's face it—there are going to be times when you aren't as prepared as you would like to be. The reasons for your lack of preparation may be beyond your control.

Sometimes interviewers like to schedule meetings with prospective employees with as little notice as possible *for the sole purpose of* seeing how well someone does under pressure. Or maybe the interview transpires from a conversation. You know, one of those 'one thing leads to another' events. That's what happened one day to Matthew…

Thirty-year-old Matthew is an accountant. He is extremely good at his job and was quickly promoted to the position of vice-president and head of accounting for a group of four large franchises of a *major* US business (all owned by the same person). He answered only to the owner of these franchises. The promotion, however, required relocating to a part of the country he and his wife had never experienced.

At first it was nice—who wouldn't like living with the beach almost at your back door, right? But after a while they realized the beauty of the landscape wasn't worth the social atmosphere. They didn't feel at home, so to speak, and they knew it was definitely not the atmosphere they wanted their two-year-old to grow up in. So, after nearly two years, Matthew decided to start looking for a position closer to home—and a lifestyle he and his wife wanted for themselves and their son.

It just so happened that while his wife's parents were visiting for a few days, they discovered that some long-time friends were also vacationing in the area at that same time. Phone calls and social media posts were exchanged and as a result, they all got together for lunch and spending the afternoon together.

The next chapter in this story 'reads' that one of these long-time friends is a very savvy and wealthy businessman. When he heard Matthew was considering changing jobs and what his qualifications and experiences were, the man offered him a job on the spot. The salary was where it should be, the benefits were great, and the location would put them almost exactly where they wanted to be.

Now before you write this off as one of those 'happily ever after' things, keep reading…

Matthew was grateful and honored for the offer, but he wasn't completely comfortable with the overall structure of the business. So, with as much tact, grace, and wisdom of someone much older, he declined the offer. The businessman was equally graceful, tactful, and wise, and no one's feelings were hurt. In fact, he went on a head-hunting website and actually made positive comments about interviewing Matthew!

Two weeks later Matthew was contacted by another major corporation who had gotten Matthew's profile and resume from that same website. The job was exactly what he was looking for in a location both he and his wife were happy about, and *now* the end of the story reads, "…and they are living happily ever after".

Matthew's off-the-cuff interview with a businessman/family friend came out of nowhere. It was totally unexpected, but because Matthew was confident in himself, his skills, and his experiences to talk about them, it all worked out just fine.

If you don't already have it, you need to develop that same sense of confidence about yourself. You need to know yourself well enough to talk about yourself with confidence at any time…any place…in any situation. To do so appropriately and effectively, think about it terms of letting the person SEE you; SEE standing for **Skills, Education** and **Experience**.

The other key components you want to be able to convey about yourself in a positive light are your abilities to **communicate,** be part of a **team-effort,** and your response to **supervision—both being supervised and working in a supervisory position.** You need to know yourself well enough to be able to answer the following questions at *any given moment.*

Communication: Your communication skills—how you handle conflict and your response to a lack of communication or miscommunication. How do you typically get your point across to others?

Teamwork: Can answer questions about leadership style, communication, attention to detail, focus, program planning, organization, etc.? How do you handle team members who drop the ball?

Supervision: Responding to changes in routine and taking on added responsibilities when asked. Management or supervision style, writing, documenting, reviewing, evaluation, and motivation.

A few last thoughts about being prepared for an interview and to talk about yourself at any given moment:

- Don't sound mechanical or rehearsed. Be genuine. Smile. Be animated (just not too animated).
- Don't be arrogant and prideful. Be truthful. Be confident, but humble.
- Remember you have a lot at stake—namely, your future.

Interview attire

Now let's move on to what you should wear to an interview. We touched on this briefly earlier in the chapter, but now let's be more specific…

There are three different categories of attire to consider when going for an interview AND going to work. And since going to work every day is the reason for the interview, it is important that you have a firm grasp on what each of these three categories looks like in your mirror.

The three categories are: **Interview attire, Professional or normal office attire,** and **Casual office attire.**

Interview Attire: What to wear for a great first impression

WOMEN

- Conservative tailored suit or dress—solid color or muted stripes.
- No bold patterns.
- Hosiery should be flesh-colored—no runs or tears.
- Pumps or flats—no boots, sandals, sneakers, casual canvas shoes, or extra-high heels.
- Little or no perfume, minimal makeup and jewelry, small handbag, (a briefcase is fine), neatly manicured nails (no bright or chipped polish and not too long) and neat, simple hairstyle.
- Body piercings and tattoos should be minimally visible or non-conspicuous.

MEN

- Solid color suit, conservative shirt and tie, leather dress shoes
- No sneakers or casual boots
- Cleanly-shaven face, trimmed nails that are clean, neatly trimmed hair.
- Body piercings and tattoos should be minimally visible or non-conspicuous.

Other general rules for interview attire include:

- Nothing too short, too tight, or too revealing
- Nothing torn, stained, or that won't stay in place when you bend, twist, or lean over

Your interview attire doesn't have to have a designer label. Hey, if you can afford *that,* do you really need the job? Just make sure you are neat, clean, and professional-looking. That's what your interviewer wants to see.

Professional and Casual Work Attire

Professional business/work attire is usually defined as a suit or slacks and sport coat for men with a button-up shirt and tie. For women, it consists of tailored suits or dresses with hosiery and flats or pumps.

Casual work attire is more loosely defined and quite honestly, it depends on the individual company or organization. In some cases, casual is jeans and a nice shirt, while in other cases, it is skirts and blouses or more casual dresses for women and jeans and button-up shirts or slacks and polos for guys.

No matter what the dress code is, however, anything too tight or revealing is always unacceptable, as is too much makeup, jewelry, perfume, and anything that is torn, stained, or ill-fitting.

The dress code is something you need to have a handle on when you accept a position with a company. But remember: it is always better to be overdressed than underdressed.

And...BREAK!

Exiting an interview is one of the most awkward situations we find ourselves in. We aren't sure what to say or how much to say. And depending on the company, it is sometimes difficult to know how or when to follow up after being interviewed.

No matter where the interview takes place or what kind of job it is, you have certain rights and responsibilities you need to assume as the interview comes to an end.

- Thank the interviewer for their time. Be sure to include a statement to the effect that you enjoyed speaking with them.
- Ask about the interviewing selection timeline. Let them know that you look forward to hearing from them and to the possibility of being a part of the company.
- Ask for one of their business cards. (if you've not already done this).

Once the interview is over and you are exiting the building, your thoughts immediately start going to places like:

- I hope he/she thought that went as well as I think it did.
- I really bombed that one.
- I'd say there's a 50-50 chance I'll be hearing anything back on that one.
- He/she said they'd let me know, but did they mean either way, or just if I get the job?
- I hope I get this job. It's just what I'm looking for.
- I'll take it if it's offered to me, but I'm not so sure it's what I want.
- I wonder how long it will be before they make a decision. They said a few days, but what's a few?

These thoughts are natural, so don't let any of them get you down or make you overly-confident. You truly are at the mercy of the prospective employer, so all you can do is wait. But while you are waiting, **be sure to write or email a thank-you note for being granted an interview.** And be sure to send the note within 24 hours.

The note should be brief, but should NOT be a form-type thank-you note. Make it personal by addressing it to the specific person who interviewed you. Also, include a comment or two about the company, the fact that you appreciated him/her asking you to share your thoughts on __________, and a humble, but direct reminder of why you would be a good fit for the job. You should end the note by saying something like, "Again, Mr. __________, I appreciate the opportunity to interview for the position of __________ and look forward to the possibility of being part of (company name).

A simple 'sincerely' or 'regards', followed by your name and contact information is the proper way to close the note.

After sending the initial thank-you note, you should wait no more or no less than two weeks to make an additional follow-up contact. This follow-up contact can be made either by email or phone call.

You should simply say that the purpose of the call or email is to inquire as to whether a decision has been made in regard to the position you interviewed for (give date, position and who interviewed you).

NOTE: The exception to this comes when you have been given specific instructions by the interviewer as to what and how contact is to be made.

If after sending the follow-up email or making the follow-up call, you receive no response, it is safe to assume you are out of the running and you should move on. I know it is difficult to be left hanging, and quite honestly, a company with integrity and strong feelings toward taking care of their employees won't do that. So....

Chapter 9:

Acceptance and Negotiation

Congratulations! You just received a phone call saying you have been chosen to come on board. You were offered the job you interviewed for a week ago and you couldn't be happier. But…

But what? Is the salary not what you were expecting? Are the benefits not actually what you thought they would be? Are you having a conflict with a start date? Relocation issues? Any one (or more) of a number of other possible issues?

When interviewing for a job, you need to go into the interview with the attitude that you will be selected to fill the position. In other words, you need to be ready to say 'yes' AND to negotiate the terms of the position.

You need to know:

- The company's basic pay scale so you will know how to negotiate your salary (if applicable).
- Specifics of the position
- Your fair market value—what the pay range is for people in your profession with similar education and experience.
- How to negotiate salary and benefits.

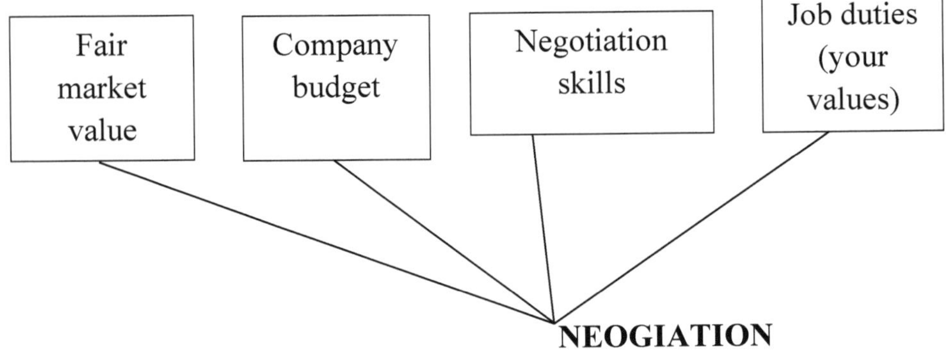

Determining your fair market value can be done by visiting websites like salary.com, payscale.com, glassdoor.com, or the Bureau of Labor Statistics website.

Additionally, you should take into consideration the cost of living in the area, your experience, and the requirements of the job. The requirements of the job will then require you to consider your values.

I've put together the following chart showing some intrinsic and extrinsic values you need to take into consideration when negotiating your job package.

INTRINSIC VALUES	EXTRINSIC VALUES
Expertise	Salary
Feel respected, treated fairly	Travel experience
Social, risk-taker, up for challenges	Vacation, health, retirement pkg.
Public contact	Set or flexible work hours
Creative and influential	Awards and recognitions
Proper work/life balance	Living environment

Reading through this chapter so far you may be asking yourself why bother? Why negotiate at all? Why not take what they offer and be happy you have a job?

In some cases, that is exactly what you need to do. If during the interview, or through your own research of the company, you know what will be offered and you are satisfied with that, then take it.

If, however, you are drawn into negotiations for salary by the interviewer or you have been pursued for a position and everything looks good *except* one or two items in the offer, then by all means, negotiate! Just be sure you do it in such a way that it **creates mutual value** for you and your employer.

Salary negotiations

Salary is the trickiest part of negotiations for a job package. Why? Because no one wants to talk about money, but everyone wants to know about money. From the employer's side of things, they want to get the most for their money while at the same time getting the best 'bargain', so to speak. From your end, you want a salary that is comparable to what you believe you are worth and what you need to live on, but you don't want to appear either too greedy or too humble. Yes, it's a tightrope to be sure, but one you must cross.

When dealing with a salary negotiation it is important to remember the following:

- Again…you want to create mutual value for you and your employer.
- You should, to the best of your ability avoid being the first one to give a figure. It is very unlikely that you'll get anything more than that.
- It isn't just about the money. Be sure you take into consideration things like how much of your health insurance they are paying, use of a company vehicle, other expense account perks, and so on.
- Don't even consider negotiating a salary until you have been offered the position. NEVER try to negotiate during an interview.

When the subject of salary negotiation comes up during an interview, try to remain somewhat vague. You can say things like:

"Could we postpone this discussion until I know more about the position?"

"For the right position, I am willing to be flexible in the beginning."

"From our discussion, I know this position has been budgeted; what is the budgeted salary range?"

Or if pressed for an answer…

"Between $45,000 and $55,000 if the assumptions I am making about others factors are accurate."

"Based on the job as described and without considering any other benefits, a salary in the mid-five figures would seem appropriate."

REMEMBER: You want to be able to factor in things you aren't quite sure of yet. Things like cost of living for the geographical location you're applying in. For example, if you're applying to a financial analyst role in St. Louis and the same job in New York City, the salary range could vary by thousands or even tens of thousands of dollars because of the cost of living in each city.

Remaining open-minded and not giving the impression that you are offended or discouraged by the offer is important. Your negotiation or counter-offer needs to come from a logical state of mind and one that will make it **mutually beneficial** to you and your employer. So once you have received the numbers and are convinced they do not meet your expectations or requirements, it is time for you to counter-offer.

When you make a counter-offer, whether it is salary-related or related to benefits, work hours, or anything else job-related, it is essential that you always present your terms in the following manner:

- ALWAYS remain professional in your attitude and behavior.
- Be patient.
- Make sure your terms are reasonable.
- Don't be intimidated by your surroundings or your employer.
- Be ready to offer compelling, logical, and verifiable reasons for your counter-offer.
- Decide beforehand if you are willing to entertain a counter to your counter-offer.
- Be ready to say yes or no to what you hear.

Knowing the dos and don'ts of making a counter-offer are one thing. Knowing HOW to make the counter-offer is another. So now let's take a look at what you need to know about that.

After you've had time to consider the original offer and have decided to try to negotiate, you need to prepare and practice what you want to say.

The first rule of negotiations is to start with the positive! Remind them what they are looking for and that you have these qualifications. You can also remind them of any additional assets you bring to the table that increases your value to the organization.

Next, don't be afraid to tactfully share the research you've done about the going wage for such positions. You might also want to give a number slightly higher than what you want; leaving room for the employer to counter your counter-offer.

I also want to reiterate that negotiation shouldn't just be about the money. There are several other negotiable factors you can bring up without even talking about your salary that will end up increasing your bottom line. Here are the major ones you need to consider when negotiating the package you are offered:

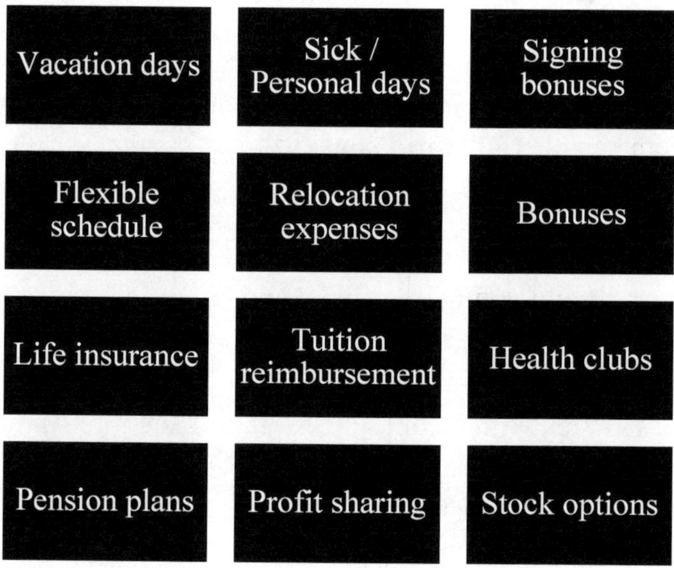

Should I take the job

In addition to salary and benefit considerations and (possible) negotiations, there are a few other things you need to take into consideration when deciding whether the job you have been offered is right for you. The following list of considerations may have been covered during the interview process, but if they weren't, you need to make sure you know what to expect regarding:

- Promotional opportunities
- Performance review? How + when
- Performance = Salary (does it)
- Salary progression timeline

The last point I want to make in talking about job offers and negotiations is something I'll call the 'juggling act'. The juggling act is the dilemma of knowing whether to accept an offer because you are still waiting to hear from someone else…and hoping you get an offer from them.

It's a good problem to have, in some respects, anyway. But having this problem can also add to an already stressful situation. And who needs that, right?

Making this decision is something only you can do. Yes, if you are married, you should definitely consult and confer with your partner, but ultimately you are the one who is going to have to decide if you are willing to risk a for-sure thing on something that isn't. You also need to be satisfied with the reasons for taking the job. And lastly, you need to realize that if you accept the job offer placed before you, it doesn't have to be your forever job. It can serve as a stepping stone to where you want to be later.

So when deciding whether to take the job…or wait for another offer, remember:

- Just because you have been given an offer, does not mean that you must accept it immediately. Express your interest and ask when they need you to give them an answer OR ask if you can have a few days to think about it?
- In that time frame, contact your "first choice" and ask about the status of your application or interview (depending on the situation). You could even tell them that you are beginning to

receive offers and you are very interested in their company. See if they can give you an idea of when you will receive notification.

- Reflect on both companies. Should your second choice actually be your first choice? IF not, will it still give what you are looking for at this time in your career?
- Make a decision. If you take the first offer, you can always reapply to your first choice later down the road. Continue to maintain the relationship with your first choice. You never know what the future holds. If you decide to decline the offer from your second choice and wait for your first choice, have NO regrets. Be confident in your decision. One company wanted you, so another one will to. Be mindful, however, that you may be waiting awhile to hear. You may also receive a decision that you do not like. Again, do NOT have any regrets. Just keep working toward your long-term goals.

Now…get out there and get the job that is right for you now and give it all you've got!

Chapter 10:
Surviving and Thriving in the First Ninety Days of Your Career

Congratulations! You got the job! You can relax now, right?

WRONG!

Yes, you can breathe that huge sigh of relief of knowing you don't have to submit another resume, wait for another call or email informing you that you have made the first cut and will be granted an interview. And yes, you can relax knowing you don't have to go through the day hoping and waiting you hear the words, "Congratulations, we feel you are the best person for the position of...."

But now you are faced with the pressure to perform. Now you must prove you *are* the best person for the job. But in going forward and taking these first steps into the real world of employment (or a new career path), remember this:

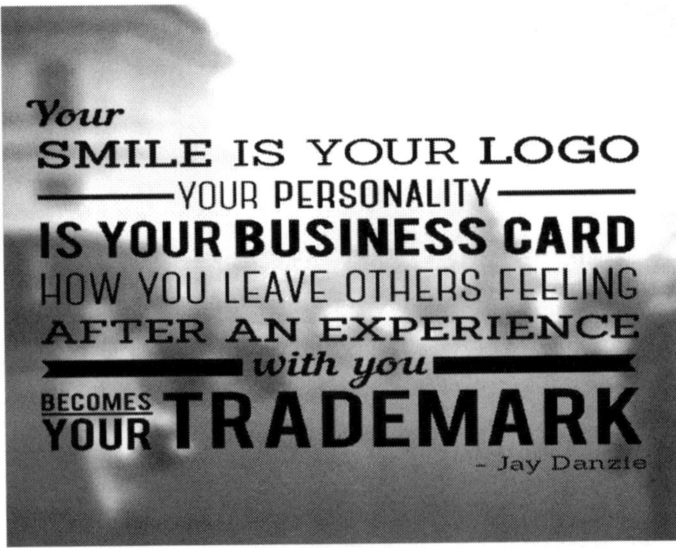

Your employer believes in you, but more importantly they are investing in you. So now it is up to you to remind them daily of why they made that initial investment and why it will continue to be a wise investment.

As time progresses and you gain additional experience, they are going to be raising their expectations of you. These increased expectations then continue to give you reasons and opportunities to showcase your **personal brand**.

FYI: If you need to be reminded of what it means to have a personal brand, go back to chapter five.

In most cases, your first ninety days of employment (or possibly longer) will be what is referred to as a probationary period or training period. During this time, it is possible that you will be working side by side with a training officer, supervisor, or a more experienced employee. This is not meant to demean or belittle your education and knowledge in your chosen field. It is simply a means most employers use to train new-hires to do things in a way that is most beneficial for their methods for doing business and the programs and operations they use.

If you are changing jobs and/or career paths, the structure of office life is not new to you. You are used to the regimen of set hours (even if flex-time is offered), specified lunch breaks, work boundaries, and office etiquette. If, however, you are fresh out of college and entering the workforce for the first time, you may be in for a shock. What's more, you may need to make some critical adjustments to your schedule and your way of thinking.

The chart on the next page outlines some typical thought processes and behavioral patterns for college students vs. working adults. Think about how you view each of them and the adjustments you need to make to make the transition successfully.

College	World of Work
Professors/Peers	Bosses /Coworkers
Structured curriculum and syllabus	Unstructured environment & tasks with little direction
Few significant changes	Frequent & unexpected changes
Flexible schedule	Structured schedule
Breaks: summer, spring, fall, winter	Vacation & sick
Personal control over time, classes, interests, etc.	Directions and interests determined by others
Faculty evaluations	Employee evaluations
Your development & growth	Organization's development & growth
Create & explore knowledge	Get results with your knowledge
Individual effort	Team effort
"Right" answers	Effective answers
Frequent, quick, & concrete feedback (grades)	Infrequent and less precise feedback

Increasing your chances for success in the workplace

Aside from giving your job 100%, there are some things you need to ALWAYS remember about being a successful member of the workforce.

#1: **Make being on time a priority.** Give yourself enough time to get to work, get coffee/breakfast and be at your desk by the beginning of your day. Likewise, make sure you leave on time or a few minutes after the end of the workday. Example: if you are scheduled to leave at 5PM, 4:55 isn't 5PM.

"Arrive a few minutes early and leave a few minutes late"—always a safe bet.

#2: **Be likeable.** This doesn't mean you must be the class (office) clown or the office doormat. It means you need to be pleasant and polite to everyone; refusing to be a part of any office drama. You need to respect the boundaries and protocol in place, and respect the 'traditions' that are in place. Be a team player. Do what you can to fit in—short of compromising your values and morals, of course.

The same holds true for your clients and customers. In today's relationship-focused, highly-connected world of work, being socially savvy is a requirement for success. Whether you are meeting people face-to-face, on the telephone, or on the computer, social skills make a big difference.

I do want to say, however, that fitting in should never require you to allow someone else to take credit for your work or to be blamed for errors you didn't make. Bridget knows first-hand how difficult fitting into the workplace can be if the environment is such that this can happen…

Bridget took a job as an assistant clerk in a small firm the summer before her junior year in college. She thought it would be a great way to prepare for law school and was excited to get some hands-on experience in her chosen field.

The three lawyers in the firm were all very helpful and amicable; giving advice, answering questions, and so forth. One of the paralegals, however, a young woman just a few years older than Bridget, went out of her way to make things difficult for her. She would leave out a detail or two when explaining an office procedure to Bridget; causing Bridget to make an error or two. She gave Bridget erroneous directions to a client's office; making her late for a meeting. She also never missed an opportunity to try to discredit Bridget in front of their bosses.

Bridget had no idea why the co-worker did these things. All she knew was that it was making her miserable, suspicious, and full of self-doubt. One day after an incident, Bridget finally asked the young woman why she was going to such great lengths to cause trouble for her. The young woman replied, "You didn't have to do anything but ask and flash your artificially-whitened teeth to get this job. I had to work hard to get here. I took online and night classes just to be a paralegal so I could support myself and my daughter. So, if you want this job you are going to have to pass a few tests to prove to me you deserve this job."

Bridget was shocked and angry. Her co-worker's life wasn't her fault! What's more, she didn't have to prove herself to anyone but her bosses. Thankfully, Bridget had the maturity and temperament to keep her emotions in check. She did, however, tell the co-worker that this wasn't a college sorority she was pledging. It was her future she was working toward. She also told her that while she hoped they could get along, she didn't have to prove herself to anyone but the lawyers they worked for.

The co-worker continued to try to sabotage Bridget, but Bridget held her ground and did so without tattling. At the end of the internship, however, Bridget did share with the lawyers everything that had taken place during the exit interview. She emphasized that her reasons for speaking up were not to cause trouble, but rather to make them aware of the fact that not only did she fulfill her duties, she did so under tremendous pressure; something she hoped they would remember when asked to be used as a reference in the future.

Bridget's experience is thankfully not the norm. But even if you do encounter a situation that is less than favorable, don't let it get to you. Don't sink to that level. Rise above it and let your personality and professionalism shine.

#3: **Dress to impress.** When you went for your interview you noticed most people were in jeans and casual shirts or another form of casual office dress. You weren't given a specific dress code, so you aren't sure how you should dress for your first day.

The answer to that is ALWAYS dress for success. You took the job, so you know what the job entails. You know whether you are going to be on a factory floor making inspections or talking to line workers. You know if you are going to be a face and voice on the front line between customers/clients and management. In other words, if a specific dress code was not provided and discussed, be safe and remember that it is always better to be overdressed than underdressed.

The important thing to remember is respect for the job. Showing a lack of concern for your personal appearance can be interpreted as a sign of disrespect to clients or co-workers and managers. Clothing that is wrinkled or worn, an unshaven face or greasy or unkempt hair conveys that you lack professionalism. Always err on the conservative side and choose your first day attire based on your position and what you have found through research to be acceptable for the job.

#4: **Understand your company's calendar and communication system.** Calendars show upcoming meetings and appointments. How do you typically schedule meetings and reminders? Cell phone, personal calendar? Those are all great ways to keep track of your appointments, but when it comes to work, you want to make sure you document those events on your work calendar. Why? Remember that you are working in a unit. It is important that your supervisor and coworkers know where you are in case they need you. Also, if a time slot seems empty, your supervisor may take that as you being available, and he or she may schedule something with you.

#5: **Be aware of and follow office etiquette.** Don't waste any time finding out what the proper office etiquette is in your new work environment.

- Is there an unspoken 'policy' that says management and subordinates don't socialize on or off the clock?
- Are their unofficial designated parking spots? You certainly don't want to end up in the boss's spot.
- What about the lunchroom? Are you expected to eat there or is it okay to go elsewhere?
- Are there office gossips you need to steer clear of? And if so, how do you do so without offending? That can be tricky, but if you are polite to everyone, you should be able to pull it off.
- Are company picnics and Christmas parties optional or mandatory (even if the mandate is assumed)?
- What about phone calls—even from your childcare provider?

You should be able to discern some of these things (and a few more I haven't mentioned) through observing your coworkers. Those you can't figure out on your own will require you to ask someone who is truly 'in the know' (not the office gossip). Whatever you do, though, be diplomatic when doing so.

For example, if asking about the office picnic, you might say, "Do most people attend the picnic? And is it family-friendly?" I think you will agree that sounds a lot better than, "What happens if I don't show up for the picnic?"

Another example of discreet questioning is this: "I don't want to take anyone's parking place by mistake, so is there any place in particular I shouldn't park? Or is it every man for himself?"

#6: **Meetings and conferences.** It's only natural for you to be somewhat nervous about attending your first meeting, presentation, or conference. You know you'll be watched and assessed on how you conduct yourself and on whether you were 'worth the hire'. So, when attending and participating in these events for the first few times, it is important that you make a positive impression and present your best self (remember your personal brand).

You also need to play it safe, as in don't assume anything. Dress professionally UNLESS you've been told otherwise. Plan to attend every seminar and then follow the lead of your boss. Be prepared to present, but don't be offended if you aren't given the opportunity to do so—even if you've done the bulk of the work. Be on time.

#7: **Attitude.** We covered the fact that you shouldn't hang with the office gossips a few paragraphs ago. Now I want to say **don't be an office gossip!** Adding to that, I'll say to you what my momma always said to me: If you can't say something nice, don't say anything at all.

Your attitude in the workplace should always be polite and respectful. Even the most obnoxious coworker deserves your respect because a) you don't know if they are going through a tough situation that is making them unpleasant and b) they might end up being your supervisor or boss someday. Hey, I'm just sayin'….

Other 'attitude boundaries you need to adhere to are:

- Don't complain about your job, the boss, coworkers, or anything else job-related.
- Avoid conversations about your personal life, politics, and money.
- Don't use foul language.
- Avoid making or taking personal calls during work hours unless absolutely necessary (and yes, we all know there are times when it is absolutely necessary).
- Don't talk badly about a previous employer or former coworkers.
- Don't expect to get promoted right away or to always receive what YOU think is the proper amount of recognition.
- Be extremely mindful of the generational differences between you and some of your coworkers and be respectful of the different mindsets you likely have about work, careers, and so forth.
- Stay true to YOUR morals and values.
- Remember that this is most likely only the first of three or more jobs in your career.
- Be neat and tidy—don't leave your work station in a mess.
- Don't misrepresent yourself. Don't be shy or afraid to share your skills, but don't claim to be more than you are.
- GET A MENTOR.
- Take advantage of every possible professional development opportunity.
- Don't let the fact that you are making a salary now (vs. paying tuition) blind you to the fact that you need to formulate and live within a budget.

#8: **Own it!** If you make a mistake, own it. Don't try to hide it, excuse it, or pass it off as someone else's mistake. You are new on the job. You aren't perfect. You are going to make a few mistakes. Everyone does. Granted, the mistakes should not be serious ones, but no one goes through their career error-free.

Don't take the previous statements as your pass or permission slip to screw up. Your goal, remember, is to do your best and prove yourself to be an asset to the company…not a liability. So in order to keep the mistakes to a bare minimum and to ensure the ones you *do* make are minor, remember to do these three things:

ASK   LISTEN LEARN

There is no such thing as a dumb question. But when you ask, don't forget to listen (and take notes, if necessary) so that you don't have to keep asking the same questions repeatedly.

#9: **Be industrious.** As a new-hire, there may be times when you feel like you are twiddling your thumbs or having too much downtime. In some jobs this is to be expected during your training period.

"Matt" knows how you feel….

During Matt's training, his supervisor keeps him engaged in a variety of tasks. Suddenly, his supervisor is called into a meeting. After an hour, Matt has completed the tasks on his list. He is bored and not sure what to do next. What would you advise Matt to do?

If I were talking to Matt, my advice to him would be that there is always work to be done. There is always something constructive you can do to fill the time when you aren't engaged with the person training you or when you have completed the tasks assigned to you and are waiting for your next set of instructions.

Here are a few suggestions for passing the time constructively:

- **Review your emails** (If your account was created prior to your start date).
    - o Create your email signature
    - o Create introduction emails if applicable
- **Ask your coworkers if they need any help or assistance.** If they don't, ask if it would be an imposition for you to observe them to learn more about what goes on in the company and how it relates to your job.
- **Read company information or orientation materials.**
- **Begin introducing yourself to other associates on your floor.**
- **Familiarize yourself with industry news specific to your company** (competition, new products, new or upcoming legislation, trade journals, etc.).
- **Seek feedback from coworkers to get a sense of what you are doing well and the areas you need to improve upon.** In those areas where you need improvement, ask for suggestions on how you can do so.
- **Seek out extra work.** Show your willingness to go above and beyond what's in the responsibilities. Volunteer for assignments that interest you and those that will enable you to use your skills and education.

Chapter 11:

Just In Case That Wasn't Enough…

Well, what do you think? I've given you a lot of information to process. I realize that, but I think you will agree it is information you need.

You need to know how to make the most of your degree—even if you choose to travel down a career path different than the one you originally planned to travel.

You need to know how to believe in yourself and why you can't expect anyone else to if you don't.

You need to know how to present yourself in the best and truest light (your personal brand).

You need to know how to establish a strong network, how to utilize that network and why networking is beneficial.

You need to know what a personal brand is, how to create yours, and how to sell it.

You need to know the in's and outs of resume and application submissions and follow-ups, as well as the other complexities of the job search process.

You need to know how to ace an interview, how to accept a job, and how to negotiate the terms of your contract.

You need to know what to do once you've signed on the dotted line and how to establish your first 'footprint' in the world of your chosen field.

And finally, you need to know how to take the leap into the other aspects of being a grown-up. You know, things like budgets, establishing credit, making major purchases, setting up retirement accounts, and more. So just in case everything you've read wasn't enough, let's take a look at how to take charge of some of these important, but non-work-related matters.

Budgets

If all I said about budgets is that you need one, that should be enough. But when I look at the fact that millennials are often faced with daunting student loan debt and are having more trouble establishing their credit than previous generations did, I think the evidence is abundantly clear that making and living within a budget is wise for both now and in the future.

There are a number of resources available to help you establish a budget that is right for you. And when I say right for you, I don't mean one that allows you to have everything you want and think you need. I mean one that allows you to live as comfortably as possible WHILE living within your means.

Before I give you a list of resources for creating a budget you can feel good about, let's talk about a few important budget-basics:

- **Save first.** Some people will refer to this as 'paying yourself'. The best way to do this is through direct-deposit. Allowing your employer to deposit money directly into your savings account and/or investment accounts is always best. You won't even miss the money because you'll never see it.
- **Take advantage of all matching contribution programs your company offers**. Example: Your employer will match up to 50% of everything you put into a deferred compensation program for your retirement. It's free money. Why wouldn't you?
- **Give/donate from off the top**. While this is typically a faith-based mindset, it is never a bad idea to donate to causes you

are passionate about on a regular basis. Planned giving builds character. Besides, these organizations are often solely reliant on donations. Being able to know they can count on a specified amount enables them to plan their outreach.

- **Following a percentage-based budget is usually the best and easiest to follow and live by.**
- **Don't deny yourself completely**. We are basically selfish creatures. We like treating ourselves. In fact, we are the masters of justification when it comes to finding excuses as to why we deserve to treat ourselves to a few little luxuries. If you don't allow a little room in your budget (and I do mean a little) for such items, you will soon find yourself cheating and even going overboard.
- **Have short and long-term budget goals**. EXAMPLES: Putting $30 a month in a vacation account so that you can take a cruise (or something you feel is special) in a couple of years is a great goal. Paying yourself $1 for every day you eat healthy and exercise so that you can get a manicure once a month or go out for dinner and a movie with friends once a month is also a fun and healthy goal to have. Driving your old car until you get your student loans paid off or until you can pay at least 40% down on a new one…SO SMART!

This list of budget resources should help you accomplish putting together a budget that meets your needs without making you feel like a child sneaking into his/her piggy bank.

https://www.free-online-calculator-use.com/budgeting-percentages-average-calculator.html

https://www.learnvest.com/knowledge-center/your-ultimate-budget-guideline-the-502030-rule/

https://christianpf.com/how-to-make-a-budget/

https://www.forbes.com/sites/financialfinesse/2012/08/29/10-common-money-management-mistakes-that-youre-probably-making/#31096e318ed3

https://www.daveramsey.com/store/financial-peace-university/financial_peace_university_lifetime_membership/prod614.html?ectid=30.36.12923&utm_source=bing&utm_medium=cpc&utm_campaign=IND%20-%20FPU%20Kit%20Sales%20-%20Bing&utm_term=financial%20peace%20university&utm_content=FPU%20Kits

BOOK: https://www.amazon.com/Millenial-Money-Fix-Boneparth-Douglas-ebook/dp/B073DFB54L/ref=sr_1_1?ie=UTF8&qid=1506107594&sr=8-1&keywords=books+about+budgeting

BOOK: https://www.amazon.com/How-Debt-Stay-Live-Prosperously-ebook/dp/B005U3ZVLK/ref=sr_1_13?ie=UTF8&qid=1506107594&sr=8-13&keywords=books+about+budgeting

Establishing credit

Along the same lines as budgeting, establishing credit is something you need to do wisely. The fact of the matter is that it is almost easier to establish bad credit than good credit. A couple of careless moves can damage your credit for years to come. Case in point:

Doug and Fiona were young newlyweds. Fiona was in school and Doug was serving in the Marine Corps. They were doing pretty well in managing things on their own until a slick car salesman talked them into a car that was really more expensive than they could comfortably afford.

Even with the hefty payments they could have made it if they wouldn't have offered to help a friend out by letting him on their cell phone plan. They should have seen the fact that he was twenty-two and couldn't get one on his own as a red flag, but they didn't. This 'friend' racked up several hundred dollars-worth of fees on the phone while overseas and left Doug and Fiona to pay for them. Their inability to do so upfront cost them hundreds more in late fees and took their credit rating to rock-bottom level.

They were able to pay the balance 'owed' within a couple of years, but it has taken four years for their credit rating to get to an acceptable level for possibly trading cars.

"It was a hard and painful experience," Fiona says. "We will never put ourselves in that position again. Ever! It has made me paranoid about spending money on anything I don't absolutely have to have. I'm almost Scrooge-like sometimes, but that's just the way it is."

When working to establish your credit, you need to keep the following in mind:

- Credit ratings tell someone whether you can be trusted with their money.
- Having a credit card isn't bad if you pay the balance IN FULL each month so as not to incur any interest charges or late fees.
- You need to establish credit to be able to purchase a home or car at the lowest possible interest rates.
- These days, even purchasing a cellphone and cellphone contract is a means of establishing credit.
- Credit can also be established by paying rent, utilities, and school loans on time.

Making major purchases

More than a few people I know reward themselves with a new car when they accept their first real job after graduating from college.

This is not a bad thing! In fact, it is often wise to get rid of the rust bucket you drove (and worked on) throughout college.

Having a dependable vehicle saves time, money, and headaches. In other words, getting a new car isn't a bad idea, as long you do it right. Neither are other major purchases such as a house or condo, or investing funds to become a partner or owner of a business—if you do it correctly.

So what is 'correctly'?

When buying a car or house, take someone with you who has had experience in such a matter. This is usually a parent. There is no shame in asking your parents for help and advice when making a major purchase. They want you to get the most for your money and they don't want you to be taken advantage of.

Shop around. Even if you end up buying the first one you look at, you need to make a few comparisons before deciding.

Do your homework.

Cars:

- Know what the insurance will be.
- Know what kind of gas mileage you can expect.
- Know what the car's safety rating is.
- Know whether it depreciates slower or faster than other cars.
- Know whether the make/model you want is 'known' for having specific problems.
- Can you afford it?

House:

- Is it in a safe neighborhood?
- How much are the taxes and insurance?
- Is it in a desirable school district?

- Is it easily-accessible in inclement weather?
- Is the roof newer and in good repair?
- Is the foundation solid?
- Is it in an area that floods easily?
- Is it an easy commute?
- Is there water damage on the walls, ceilings, attic, or under the sinks?
- Are the steps strong and sturdy?
- Do appliances stay? Are they in good working order?
- Does everything about the house meet with city codes?
- Can you afford it?

Doug and Fiona (remember them?) were halfway across the country from Fiona's parents when they purchased their car. Both say they will never purchase a vehicle or make any other major purchase without Fiona's parents' input and advice.

Clint and Maggie feel the same way. Clint makes a six-figure salary doing what he does best—accounting. But when it comes to fixing things around the house or knowing what to look for when buying a house, he admits he is nowhere near as savvy as he needs to be. That's why when he and Maggie bought a home, they took Maggie's parents with them to look it over before making an offer. They knew if the home passed their inspection and approval, it would be a great place to raise their family and grow old together.

Angela was single and fresh out of nursing school. She wanted a new car, so she called up her dad and asked him to spend the day with her car shopping and making the best deal. Dinner, she said, would be her treat.

They had a great time together and Angela drove away with a new car she loved (and is still driving her kids around in nine years later).

As for investing in a business (either as a partner or owner), you will need to follow and adhere to the requirements of your lending institution. Additionally, you need to:

- Seek legal counsel to know whether the contract is in order and covers all the necessary bases.
- Understand the contract—what it entitles you to and what responsibilities and liabilities you have.
- Know beyond a reasonable doubt that the business you are entering into will be a wise investment and venture if managed wisely and properly.
- Feel confident in your ability to trust those you are going into business with.
- Know what grants and low-interest loans are available to you.
- Have an escape plan if things don't go as planned. And yes, you always need a PLAN B.

The following resources can help you in making these decisions:

https://www.forbes.com/sites/work-in-progress/2014/06/13/5-questions-to-ask-before-going-into-business-with-a-friend/#169de7214af9

https://www.legalzoom.com/sem/biz/llc.html?kid=d542af6c-762c-4cca-b13b-31834e0331fc&utm_source=bing&utm_medium=cpc&utm_term=starting_an_llc&utm_content=d542af6c-762c-4cca-b13b-31834e0331fc&utm_campaign=BIZ_|_LLC

https://www.usagrantapplications.org/small_business_grants.php

Your state's small business association and the federal small business association will also be a tremendous help to you, as well.

Setting up retirement accounts and understanding health insurance

Healthcare and retirement accounts are something most companies offer as part of their benefit package. Because it is part of the company's benefit package, the HR department will be able to guide you through some of this by explaining what the different options involve. But they shouldn't be your sole source of advisement. Remember, it's their job to tell you what your options are. It is NOT their job to advise you which options are right for you.

Once again, seek out the advice of someone who has had experience in these matters. If you have other investments, seek counsel from your financial advisor. If you don't, but your parents, spouse, or siblings, do, ask them to put you in contact with their financial advisor. From there you can choose one of your own.

It is important that you take the time to read through the literature that defines and describes the benefits you are entitled to. You also need to be familiar with the processes for making claims, drawing out funds, filing the proper paperwork, and any yearly deadlines that may apply to the various benefits. Not knowing these things can prove to be costly—both in terms of money and your health and wellbeing.

Remember: Benefits are meant to be used to YOUR benefit.

Growing up and becoming an adult living in an adult world is something you've been working toward since the day you were born. Now that you are finally here, there are going to be times when you look at yourself and say, "I did it and I'm ready to make my mark!" And then there are going to be times when you want to tuck your tail and run straight back to your childhood—to the time when life was easier.

We both know you can't turn back time though, so it is my hope that in reading this book you now feel better equipped to move forward and to do it successfully. Oh, and by success, I mean that you will do so sharing the wisdom, wit and intellect, and charm that is YOUR Y!

FINAL WORD

GREAT JOB! By completing this book, you have taken many steps in preparing for your next professional opportunity.

What's next you may ask? What's next is that you take the resources, guidance, and advice that were hopefully gained through this book and continue to apply it to your daily life.

You are a STRONG, BEAUTIFUL, and CONFIDENT individual. The world deserves to know you and your talents and skills. Please do NOT let the day-to-day stressors of life make you doubt your worth or feel less empowered. Remember, although defeat and adversity is inevitable, you have the POWER and RESILENCE to keep pushing forward to reach your "Y."

For additional information about the author or to receive individualized job and professional development services please go to:

https://www.tnorthcareerconsulting.com/

CAREER RESOURCES

Job Search

1. LinkedIn. https://www.linkedin.com/

2. Indeed. https://www.indeed.com/

3. Glassdoor. https://www.glassdoor.com/index.htm

4. Monster. https://www.monster.com/

5. Simply Hired. https://www.simplyhired.com/

6. CareerBuilder. https://www.careerbuilder.com/

7. Robert Half. https://www.roberthalf.com/

8. TheLadders. https://www.theladders.com/

9. USAJOBS. https://www.usajobs.gov/

10. ZipRecruiter. https://www.ziprecruiter.com/

Career Research

1. Occupational Outlook Handbook. https://www.bls.gov/ooh/

2. O*NET Online. https://www.onetonline.org/

Salary

1. LinkedIn Salary. https://www.linkedin.com/salary/

2. Glassdoor Salary.
    https://www.glassdoor.com/Salaries/index.htm

3. Salary.com. https://www.salary.com/

4. PayScale. https://www.payscale.com/salary-calculator

Professional Development Webinars

1. Personal Branding and Networking
https://www.youtube.com/watch?v=keKBsu1cUAw

2. Career Exploration and Re-transitioning
https://www.youtube.com/watch?v=q8aIbbr5Hrg

ACKNOWLEDGEMENTS

Similar to the job search, writing this book was a lengthy process that involved a lot of people and a lot of support. Writing a book that focused on helping others is truly my passion and something that I have always wanted to do. I would like to take the opportunity to thank those individuals who have given me the strength and support to pursue one of my dreams:

God- I could not have made it this far in my life without your love and guidance. Thank you for always protecting me and helping me overcome the challenges that I faced.

My Husband- You are my rock and my everything. Thank you for believing in me and pushing me through my moments of self-doubt.

Mom- Thank you for everything! Because of you, I am who I am today. Thank you for making me see my worth and always recognizing my true potential.

Dad- You have always challenged me to be the best that I could be. Thank you for always motivating me and being someone I could always go to for advice and guidance.

Carol- Thank you for always loving me as your daughter. You have always been so supportive and someone that I could always turn to in times of need. Your fun-loving spirit is very contagious and a characteristic that I have always admired.

Grandma Georgia- You are the reason that I could write a book such as this one. Thank you for passing down your amazing writing ability and communication skills. There is not a day that goes by that I do not think of you. I miss you very much.

Grandmother Jewell- You are one of the sweetest and fun-loving people that I know. Thank you for your kind spirit and always supporting me in everything that I do.

My friends- There are so many of you who have had a positive influence in my life. Words cannot express how much your friendship means to me. Thank you for allowing me to enjoy life to the fullest and being there when I needed someone to talk to.

Darla- Thank you so much for being a sounding board and a mentor with writing this book. I could not have accomplished this goal without your knowledge and expertise. Your vision for this book is more than I could have ever imagined.

Finally, thank you to all of you who purchased this book and/or attended any of my presentations, workshops, or classes. You are truly a part of my "Y" and the inspiration for following my dreams. I could not have done this without you.

NOTES

Chapter 1

1. Brooks, Katharine. *You Majored in What?: Mapping Your Path from Chaos to Career*. New York: Viking, 2010.
2. Shakespeare, William. *Romeo and Juliet.* Act II. Scene II.

Chapter 2

1. Bump, Philip. "Here Is When Each Generation Begins and Ends, According to Facts." *The Atlantic*, Atlantic Media Company, 4 Oct. 2016, www.theatlantic.com/national/archive/2014/03/here-is-when-each-generation-begins-and-ends-according-to-facts/359589/.
2. "Generational Differences Chart ." *Generational Differences Chart* , www.wmfc.org/uploads/GenerationalDifferencesChart.pdf.

Chapter 3

1. Brooks, Katharine. *You Majored in What?: Mapping Your Path from Chaos to Career*. New York: Viking, 2010.
2. "Career Counseling Library." Clinical Depression | University Health Services. Accessed June 07, 2018. https://uhs.berkeley.edu/career-library.
3. K. Brooks. "Possible Lives Map." Possible Lives Map. 2010. Accessed June 7, 2018. https://www2.humboldt.edu/acac/sites/default/files/u27/Possible Lives Map Lesson Plan.pdf.

4. "UC Berkeley Career Center | Career Center." Career Clarity: Career Exploration | Career Center. Accessed June 07, 2018. https://career.berkeley.edu/.

5. "Work." Merriam-Webster. Accessed June 07, 2018. https://www.merriam-webster.com/dictionary/work.

Chapter 4

1. "Glassdoor Job Search | Find the Job That Fits Your Life." Glassdoor. Accessed June 07, 2018. https://www.glassdoor.com/index.htm.

2. LinkedIn. Accessed June 07, 2018. https://www.linkedin.com/.

3. "Twitter. It's What's Happening." Twitter. Accessed June 07, 2018. https://twitter.com/.

Chapter 5

1. Admin. "Dunkin Donuts Logo." Illionis Home. January 29, 2018. Accessed June 07, 2018. http://illinoisdouble.com/dunkin-donuts-logo/.

2. "Be Relevant, Be Memorable and Be Noticed with a Marketing Message." Career Attraction. August 16, 2017. Accessed June 07, 2018. https://www.careerattraction.com/be-relevant-be-memorable-and-be-noticed-with-a-marketing-message/.

3. "Coca-Cola." Peanuts Wiki. Accessed June 07, 2018. http://peanuts.wikia.com/wiki/Coca-Cola.

4. DeMers, Jayson. "The 7 Basic Principles That Dictate Content Marketing Success." The Huffington Post. August 12, 2017. Accessed June 07, 2018. https://www.huffingtonpost.com/jayson-demers/the-7-basic-principles-th_b_11432784.html.

5. James, Geoffrey. "20 Epic Fails in Global Branding." Inc.com. October 29, 2014. Accessed June 07, 2018. https://www.inc.com/geoffrey-james/the-20-worst-brand-translations-of-all-time.html.

6. (https://medianique.nl), MEDIANIQUE. "Nautica Logo." GoodLogo. Accessed June 07, 2018. https://goodlogo.com/extended.info/nautica-logo-3235.

7. "M&M's Font." Font Meme. Accessed June 07, 2018. https://fontmeme.com/mms-font/.

8. "Target Logo PNG Transparent & SVG Vector." Freebie Supply. Accessed June 07, 2018. https://freebiesupply.com/logos/target-logo/.

9. Tide Logo. Accessed June 07, 2018. http://www.fetchlogos.com/fmcg-logos/tide-logo/.

Chapter 6

1. "Build Your Future with O*NET OnLine." O*NET OnLine. Accessed June 07, 2018. https://www.onetonline.org/.

2. "Home : Occupational Outlook Handbook:." U.S. Bureau of Labor Statistics. April 13, 2018. Accessed June 07, 2018. https://www.bls.gov/ooh/.

3. "What Is Networking and How Does It Help You Find a Job?" Vault. Accessed June 07, 2018. http://www.vault.com/networking/article/networking/what-is-networking-and-how-does-it-help-you-find-a-job.

Chapter 7

1. "16 Job Search Behaviors That Are Causing You Unnecessary Stress." Idealist Careers. April 14, 2015. Accessed June 07, 2018. https://idealistcareers.org/16-job-search-behaviors-that-are-causing-you-unnecessary-stress/.

2. "Career Services." SLU Ride Program : Saint Louis University Facilities Services : SLU. Accessed June 07, 2018. https://www.slu.edu/life-at-slu/career-services.

3. "Glassdoor Job Search | Find the Job That Fits Your Life." Glassdoor. Accessed June 07, 2018. https://www.glassdoor.com/index.htm.

4. "How Stress Affects Your Body and Behavior." Mayo Clinic. April 28, 2016. Accessed June 07, 2018. https://www.mayoclinic.org/healthy-lifestyle/stress-management/in-depth/stress-symptoms/art-20050987.

5. Hu, James. "8 Things You Need To Know About Applicant Tracking Systems." Jobscan Blog. May 12, 2018. Accessed June 07, 2018. https://www.jobscan.co/blog/8-things-you-need-to-know-about-applicant-tracking-systems/.

6. "Job Search | Indeed." Jobs. Accessed June 07, 2018. https://www.indeed.com/.

7. LinkedIn. Accessed June 07, 2018. https://www.linkedin.com/.

Chapter 8

1. "Attire." The Balance Careers. Accessed June 07, 2018. https://www.thebalancecareers.com/interview-attire-4161908.

2. "Career Services." SLU Ride Program : Saint Louis University Facilities Services : SLU. Accessed June 07, 2018. https://www.slu.edu/life-at-slu/career-services.

3. Eilers, Christian. "65 Best Questions to Ask an Interviewer & Land Top Jobs [Proven Tips]." Resume Builder Online: Your Resume Ready in 5 Minutes! April 03, 2018. Accessed June 07, 2018. https://uptowork.com/blog/questions-to-ask-an-interviewer.

4. "How to Give a STAR Performance in a CB Interview." I Want My Career. April 15, 2015. Accessed June 07, 2018. http://iwantmycareer.com/give-star-performance-cb-interview/.

5. "Job Search Resources." SLU Ride Program : Saint Louis University Facilities Services : SLU. Accessed June 07, 2018. https://www.slu.edu/business/career-resources-center/job-search-resources.php.

6. Lively, Nathan. "Interview Tips For Sound Engineers - The S.T.A.R. Technique." Sound Design Live. August 16, 2013. Accessed June 07, 2018.

https://www.sounddesignlive.com/interview-tips-sound-engineers-star-technique/.

Chapter 9

1. "AAUW Is Training 10 Million Women to Negotiate Their Financial Futures by 2022." AAUW Salary Negotiation Programs. Accessed June 08, 2018. https://salary.aauw.org/.

2. "Career Services." SLU Ride Program : Saint Louis University Facilities Services : SLU. Accessed June 07, 2018. https://www.slu.edu/life-at-slu/career-services/index.php.

Chapter 10

1. Callum, Ian. "The Secret to Surviving the First 90 Days of Your New Job." LinkedIn. February 02, 2015. Accessed June 08, 2018. https://www.linkedin.com/pulse/secret-surviving-first-90-days-your-new-job-ian-callum/.

2. Oregon State Career Services. "Transitioning from College to the Workplace." Transitioning from College to the Workplace. Accessed June 8, 2018. http://career.oregonstate.edu/sites/career.oregonstate.edu/files/transitioning_from_college_to_workplace.pdf.

3. Quora. "18 Useful Tips For Your First 90 Days Of Any New Job." Forbes. May 01, 2015. Accessed June 08, 2018. https://www.forbes.com/sites/quora/2015/05/01/18-useful-tips-for-your-first-90-days-of-any-new-job/#3652bcc22620.

4. Tag Team Design. "How Quality Graphic Design Can Strengthen Your Brand." Tag Team Design. September 15, 2016. Accessed June 08, 2018. https://www.tagteamdesign.com/quality-graphic-design-can-strengthen-brand-2.

Chapter 11

1. Bob. "How To Make A Simple Budget." SeedTime. January 16, 2012. Accessed June 08, 2018. https://christianpf.com/how-to-make-a-budget/.

2. Boneparth, Douglas A., and Heather Boneparth. *The Millennial Money Fix: What You Need to Know about Budgeting, Debt, and Finding Financial Freedom*. Wayne, NJ: Career Press, 2017.

3. "Budgeting Percentages Average Calculator: Budget Based On Income." Free-Online-Calculator-Use.com. Accessed June 08, 2018. https://www.free-online-calculator-use.com/budgeting-percentages-average-calculator.html.

4. Carter, Erik. "10 Common Money Management Mistakes That You're Probably Making." Forbes. November 29, 2012. Accessed June 08, 2018. https://www.forbes.com/sites/financialfinesse/2012/08/29/10-common-money-management-mistakes-that-youre-probably-making/#31096e318ed3.

5. "Financial Peace University." Daveramsey.com. Accessed June 08, 2018. https://www.daveramsey.com/store/financial-

peace-university/financial_peace_university_lifetime_membership/ prod614.html?ectid=30.36.12923&utm_source=bing&utm_ medium=cpc&utm_campaign=IND - FPU Kit Sales - Bing&utm_term=financial peace university&utm_content=FPU Kits.

6. "Form an LLC Online." Legalzoom.com. Accessed June 08, 2018. https://www.legalzoom.com/sem/biz/llc.html?kid=d542af6c-762c-4cca-b13b-31834e0331fc&utm_source=bing&utm_medium=cpc&utm_t erm=starting_an_llc&utm_content=d542af6c-762c-4cca-b13b-31834e0331fc&utm_campaign=BIZ_|_LLC.

7. "Grant Applications Are Available Now for Small Business Owners." USA Grant Applications. Accessed June 08, 2018. https://www.usagrantapplications.org/small_business_grants. php.

8. LearnVest. "How to Budget Your Money With the 50/20/30 Guideline." LearnVest - Financial Planning Services and Personal Finance News. June 30, 2014. Accessed June 08, 2018. https://www.learnvest.com/knowledge-center/your-ultimate-budget-guideline-the-502030-rule/.

9. Mundis, Jerrold J. *How to Get out of Debt, Stay out of Debt, and Live Prosperously* *(based on the Proven Principles and Techniques of Debtors Anonymous)*. New York: Bantam Books Trade Paperbacks, 2012.

10. Rezvani, Selena. "5 Questions To Ask Before Going Into Business With A Friend." Forbes. July 31, 2014. Accessed June 08, 2018.

ABOUT THE AUTHOR

Jordan M. Watson is a Licensed Professional Counselor, Career Consultant, and Etiquette Consultant. She received her Bachelor of Arts and Science in Journalism with a concentration in Public Relations from Georgia State University and a Master of Education in Clinical Mental Health Counseling from the University of Missouri- St. Louis. Jordan has nearly a decade of experience presenting professional development workshops and coaching college students and young and experienced professionals. She is also certified in the DISC Assessment and Myers Briggs Type Indicator, which has strengthened her counseling and coaching experience.

INDEX

A

Angela, 187
Attire
>interview, 158-159
>workplace, 175

B

Branding
>visibility, 73-74
>consistency, 74-76
>originality, 76-77
>fit, 77-78
>bad branding
>examples, 77-78
>building, 78-79
>advertising, 79-81
>networking, 107
>workplace, 171
Bridget, 173-175
Budget, 182-184
Bullock, Sandra, 120-121

C

Clint and Maggie, 187
College vs. world of work, 172
Company websites
>research, 65
>networking, 102
Cover letters, *See resume and cover letter*
Credit, 184-185

D

Darcy, 69
Deanna, 86
Definition of work
>notes, 42
>self and work, 43-46
>work and life, 46-47
Degree
>degree activity, 11-13
>marketing yourself, 20-21
Doug and Fiona, 184 &187
Doug and Lucy, 101

E

Elizabeth, 33
Elizabeth and John, 88-89
Emily P. 18- 20
Eric and Susan, 97-98
Exploration
>as change, 31
>versus irresponsibility, 31-32
>when unnecessary, 32-33
Exploring Your Options
activity, 34-39

F

Franklin and Kelly, 45-46
Future State of You
activity, 56

G

Gene and Ben, 91
Generation descriptions
>Greatest Generation, 22-23
>Baby Boomers, 23-25
>Generation X, 25
>Millennials, 26-27

Glassdoor
    research, 66
    job search, 124
Goals
    The Present State of You activity, 52-56
    job search, 122-123
    interview question, 145
Gwen, 98-99

I
Interviewing
    Job search, 118
    preparation, 137-139
    types, 140-142
    first impression, 143
    body language, 144
    interviewer questions, 144-152
    interviewee questions, 153
    communication, 156
    teamwork, 156
    supervision, 156
    attire, 157-159
    follow-up, 161
Interests
    The Present State of You activity, 53
    research, 61
    networking, 104

J
Jared and Christopher, 20-21
Job application reminders, 132
Job search
    self-care essentials, 116-117
    stressors, 117-119
    coping strategies, 121-125
    reflection activity, 133-135
Jordan, 121

K
Katy, 88

L
Lauren and Rebecca, 93-94
LinkedIn,
    research, 67
    job search, 124
Logos, 70-72

M
Major purchases, 185-188
Mapping My Life activity, 50-51
Mapping Your Major activity, 15-17
Mark, 87-88
Marketing message
    formal vs. informal, 80
    description, 80-81
    outline, 82-83
    networking, 106-107
    resume and cover letter, 130

Marley, 92-93
Matt, 179
Matthew, 96
Matthew, 154-155
Michelle, 73-74
My Personal Timeline activity, 48-49

N

Networking
research, 67, 105-107
elements, 85-90
case examples, 91-94
strategies, 95-102
preparation, 102-108
worksheet, 109-112
notes,113
job search, 123-124

O
Olivia, 28-31

P
Personal branding, *see
branding*
Personal marketing message,
see marketing message
Personal mission statement,
58-59

Q
Qualifications
branding, 79
networking, 103
R
Research
companies, 64-66
Resume and cover letter
components, 125-130
marketing message,130
tailoring, 130-131
Applicant Tracking
System, 130-131
Retirement and health
insurance, 189

S
Salary negotiation

intrinsic vs. extrinsic
values, 163
delay techniques, 164-
165
counter-offer, 166-167
juggling act, 168-169
SEE approach, 155
"Social Media Syndrome
definition, 7
job search, 117
Self-care
definition, 115
essentials, 116
Skills
The Present State Of You
activity, 52
marketing message, 80
branding, 82
STAR Story approach, 148-
152
Steve, 67-68
Strengths
branding, 78
networking, 103
interview question, 145
Success in the workplace,
173-178

T
The Present State of You
activity, 52-56

V
Values
workplace, 53
branding, 78
networking, 102-103
intrinsic vs.
extrinsic,163

W
Weaknessess
 The Present State of You, 55
 interview question, 145
Who I Want to Be activity, 57
William Shakespeare, 10